First World War
and Army of Occupation
War Diary
France, Belgium and Germany

15 DIVISION
44 Infantry Brigade,
Brigade Machine Gun Company
1 March 1916 - 28 February 1918

WO95/1941/2

The Naval & Military Press Ltd
www.nmarchive.com
Published in association with The National Archives

Published by

The Naval & Military Press Ltd

Unit 10 Ridgewood Industrial Park,

Uckfield, East Sussex,

TN22 5QE England

Tel: +44 (0) 1825 749494

www.naval-military-press.com

www.nmarchive.com

This diary has been reprinted in facsimile from the original. Any imperfections are inevitably reproduced and the quality may fall short of modern type and cartographic standards.

Contents

Document type	Place/Title	Date From	Date To
Heading	WO95/1941/2 1916 May-1918 Feb No 44 Brigade Machine Gun Company		
Heading	15th Division 44th Infy Bde 44th Machine Gun Coy. Mar 1916-Feb 1918		
War Diary	War Diary For The Month Of March 1916. Volume. 44 M.G Coy		
War Diary	Magingarbe	01/03/1916	02/03/1916
War Diary	Goenay	03/03/1916	07/03/1916
War Diary	Magingarbe	08/03/1916	19/03/1916
War Diary	Hoeux-Les-Mines.	20/03/1918	24/03/1918
War Diary	Magingarbe	25/03/1916	01/04/1916
War Diary	Allouagne	02/04/1916	07/04/1916
War Diary	Febvin Palfart	08/04/1916	08/04/1916
War Diary	Allouagne	09/04/1916	30/04/1916
Heading	War Diary For the month of May 1916 Cmdg. No. 44 Machine Gun Company		
War Diary	Noyelles	01/05/1916	10/05/1916
War Diary	Bethune	11/05/1916	18/05/1916
War Diary	Vermelles	19/05/1916	31/05/1916
War Diary	No 44 Bde. M.G. Coy. War Diary For The Month Of June 1916 Volume 5 44 M.G. Coy Vol 4		
War Diary	Vermelles	01/06/1916	03/06/1916
War Diary	Noyelles	04/06/1916	30/06/1916
Heading	No 44 Machine Gun Company War Diary For The Month Of July 1916 Vol 5		
Miscellaneous	To Headquarters 44th Infantry Bde.		
War Diary	Novelles	01/07/1916	05/07/1916
War Diary	Vermelles	05/07/1916	22/07/1916
War Diary	Noeux Les Mines	23/07/1916	23/07/1916
War Diary	La Thieuloye	24/07/1916	26/07/1916
War Diary	Averdoingt	27/07/1916	27/07/1916
War Diary	Remaisnil	28/07/1916	28/07/1916
War Diary	Gezaine Court	29/07/1916	31/07/1916
Heading	44th Brigade 15th Division 44 Brigde Machine Gun Company August 1916		
War Diary	No. 44 Machine Gun Coy War Diary For The Month Of August 1916		
War Diary	Wargnies.	01/08/1916	04/08/1916
War Diary	Mirvaux	05/08/1916	05/08/1916
War Diary	Behencourt	06/08/1916	08/08/1916
War Diary	Albert	09/08/1916	13/08/1916
War Diary	Contalmaison	14/08/1916	26/08/1916
Diagram etc	15th Division Special Operation Map No. 13/8/16		
War Diary	Contalmaison	27/08/1916	29/08/1916
War Diary	Albert	30/08/1916	31/08/1916
Heading	No 44. Machine Gun Company War Diary For The Month Of September 1916 Volume 7		
War Diary	Albert	01/09/1916	04/09/1916
War Diary	Lonely Trench	05/09/1916	05/09/1916
War Diary	Mametz Wood	06/09/1916	10/09/1916

War Diary	Shelter Wood	11/09/1916	11/09/1916
War Diary	Lonely Trench	12/09/1916	13/09/1916
War Diary	Albert	14/09/1916	14/09/1916
War Diary	Lonely Trench	15/09/1916	17/09/1916
War Diary	Pioneer Redoubt	18/09/1916	18/09/1916
War Diary	Albert	19/09/1916	19/09/1916
War Diary	Lavieville	20/09/1916	20/09/1916
War Diary	Frhdivillers	21/09/1916	30/09/1916
War Diary	Confidential War Diary of 44. Coy M.G. Corps From 1/10/16 To 31/10/16 Volume IX		
War Diary	Franvillers	01/10/1916	05/10/1916
War Diary	Becourt	06/10/1916	08/10/1916
War Diary	Bazentin	09/10/1916	31/10/1916
Miscellaneous	Indirect Fire Targets.		
Heading	Confidential War Diary Of. 44 Coy M. Gun Corps From 1st November To 30th November 1916 Volume 9		
War Diary	Bazentin	01/11/1916	03/11/1916
War Diary	Becourt	04/11/1916	06/11/1916
War Diary	Bresle	06/11/1916	27/11/1916
Miscellaneous	Programme Of Work		
Miscellaneous	Programme Of Training No. 1916		
Miscellaneous	Special Classes Nov 20-25		
Miscellaneous	Programme Of Work		
War Diary	Confidential War Diary of 44th Machine Gun Company From December 1st 1916 To December 30th 1916 (Volume XI)		
War Diary	Albert	01/12/1916	15/12/1916
War Diary	Shelter Wood	18/12/1916	18/12/1916
War Diary	Martin Puich	19/12/1916	27/12/1916
War Diary	Shelter Wood	28/12/1916	30/12/1916
Miscellaneous	44 M.G. Coy Programme Of Work	16/12/1916	16/12/1916
Miscellaneous	44 M.G. Coy Programme Of Work		
Operation(al) Order(s)	Operation Order No. 1	29/11/1916	29/11/1916
Heading	Confidential War Diary 44th Machine Gun Company From January 1st 1917 to January 31st 1917 (Volume XII)		
War Diary	Pioneer Camp	01/01/1917	08/01/1917
War Diary	Shelter Wood	09/01/1917	10/01/1917
War Diary	AGO Drop Camp	12/01/1917	19/01/1917
War Diary	Shelter Wood	20/01/1917	23/01/1917
War Diary	Pioneer Camp	24/01/1917	31/01/1917
Operation(al) Order(s)	Operation Order No. 4. By Major R King Commanding No. 144 Gun Coy. War Diary.		
Operation(al) Order(s)	Operation Order No. 5. By Major C. King Commanding No. 44. M.G. Coy Friday 11 Jan 1917	11/01/1917	11/01/1917
Operation(al) Order(s)	Operation Order No. 6 by Major C. King Commanding No 44 M.Gun Company	16/01/1917	16/01/1917
War Diary	Operation Order No. 7 by Major C. King Commanding No 44 M.Gun Company	20/01/1917	20/01/1917
Operation(al) Order(s)	Operation Order No. 8 by Major C. King Commanding No 44 Machine Gun Coy Warm Diary	24/01/1917	24/01/1917
Operation(al) Order(s)	Operation Order No. 9 by Major C. King Commanding No 44 Machine Gun Company Warm Diary	26/01/1917	26/01/1917
Operation(al) Order(s)	Operation Order No. 10 by Major C. King Commanding No 44 Machine Gun Coy Warm Diary	28/01/1917	28/01/1917
Heading	War Diary		

Operation(al) Order(s)	Operation Order No. 11 by Major C. King. Commanding No 44 M.G. Coy War Diary	29/01/1917	29/01/1917
Operation(al) Order(s)	Operation Order No. 12 by Major C. King. Commanding No 44 M.G. Coy War Diary	31/01/1917	31/01/1917
Heading	Confidential War Diary of 44th Machine Gun Company From 1st January 1917 to 28th January 1917 Vol XIII		
War Diary	Becourt Wood	01/02/1917	03/02/1917
War Diary	Vadencourt	04/02/1917	13/02/1917
War Diary	Beauval	14/02/1917	14/02/1917
War Diary	Gezaincourt	15/02/1917	15/02/1917
War Diary	Fortel	16/02/1917	16/02/1917
War Diary	Hericourt	17/02/1917	17/02/1917
War Diary	Ocoche	18/02/1917	20/02/1917
War Diary	Lucheux	21/02/1917	22/02/1917
War Diary	Halloy	23/02/1917	27/02/1917
War Diary	Bailleuval	28/02/1917	28/02/1917
Operation(al) Order(s)	Operation Order No. 13 By Major C. King Commanding No 44 M.G. Coy.War Diary App I		
Miscellaneous	44th M.G. Coy. Programme Of Training For Week Ended 10th Feb 1917	10/02/1917	10/02/1917
Operation(al) Order(s)	Operation Order No. 14. By Lieut K.V. Barrett. App III	14/02/1914	14/02/1914
Operation(al) Order(s)	Operation Order No. 16. By Lieut K V. Barrett. Commanding No. 44 M.G.Coy App V		
Operation(al) Order(s)	Operation Order No. 17 By Lieut K.V. Barrett. App VI	17/02/1917	17/02/1917
Operation(al) Order(s)	Operation Order No. 18 By Lieut K.V. Barrett. Commanding No 44 M.G Coy 16th Feb 1917 App VII	18/02/1917	18/02/1917
Operation(al) Order(s)	Operation Order No. 18. By Lieut K.V. Barrett. Commanding No. 44 M.G Coy 18th Feb 1917 App Vii	18/02/1917	18/02/1917
Operation(al) Order(s)	Operation Order No. 18. By Lieut K.V. Barrett. Commanding No. 44 M.G Coy 18th Feb 1917 App Vii	15/02/1917	15/02/1917
Operation(al) Order(s)	Operation Order No.19 By Major C. King. Commanding No 44 M.Gun Coy. War Diary App VIII`	21/02/1917	21/02/1917
Miscellaneous	Distribution		
Operation(al) Order(s)	Operation Order No 20 Major C King Commanding No 44 M.G Coy App IX	23/02/1917	23/02/1917
Miscellaneous	Distribution		
Operation(al) Order(s)	Operation Order No.21. By Major C. King. App X	28/02/1917	28/02/1917
Miscellaneous	Distribution		
War Diary	Confidential War Diary 44 Machine Gun Company From 1st March 1917 To 31st March 1917 Volume XIV		
War Diary	Fermont	01/03/1917	18/03/1917
War Diary	Blaireville	19/03/1917	19/03/1917
War Diary	Fermont	20/03/1917	21/03/1917
War Diary	Duisans	22/03/1917	29/03/1917
War Diary	Arras	30/03/1917	31/03/1917
War Diary	Operation Order No. 22 By Major C King. App 1	01/03/1917	01/03/1917
Operation(al) Order(s)	Operation Order No. 22 By Major C King. Commanding No 44 M.G. Coy War Diary App 2	05/03/1917	05/03/1917
Operation(al) Order(s)	Addendum No. 1 De O.O. 23 Ref Beaumetz 10000 I A		
Miscellaneous	A Form. Messages And Signals.		
Operation(al) Order(s)	Operation Order No. 25. By Major C King. App 3 Commanding No 44 M.G. Coy.	18/03/1917	18/03/1917
Operation(al) Order(s)	O.O. No. 25 (Cent)		
Operation(al) Order(s)	Operation Order No. 26. By Major C King Commanding No 44 M.G. Coy. App 4	19/03/1917	19/03/1917

Operation(al) Order(s)	Operation Order No. 27 By Major C King Comdg. No. 44 M.G. Coy App 5	22/03/1917	22/03/1917
Operation(al) Order(s)	Addendum No. 1 O.O. No. 27	21/03/1917	21/03/1917
Operation(al) Order(s)	Operation Order No. 28 By Major C. King Comdg. No. 44 M.G. Coy. App 6	30/03/1917	30/03/1917
Heading	44 MGC. April 1917		
Heading	15th Div Artillery		
Heading	Confidential War Diary of 44th Machine Gun Company From April 1st 1917 to April 30th 1917 (Volume XV)		
War Diary	Arras	01/04/1917	30/04/1917
Miscellaneous	To A.R. Ref. BM. 28	01/05/1917	01/05/1917
Miscellaneous	Statement of Next taken by 44 Machine Gun Company. In The Operation From 19th-29th April	02/05/1917	02/05/1917
Miscellaneous	Points Noticed Surrey the Operation	01/05/1917	01/05/1917
Miscellaneous	Preliminary Instruction for Offensive Operations	03/04/1917	03/04/1917
Miscellaneous	Addendum No. 1 Preliminary Instruction For Offensive Operation.	05/04/1917	05/04/1917
Operation(al) Order(s)	Operation Order No. 29 By Major. C. King. Comdg. 44th M.G. Coy. 8th April 1917	08/04/1917	08/04/1917
Operation(al) Order(s)	Addendum No. 1 To O.O. No. 29	08/04/1917	08/04/1917
Operation(al) Order(s)	Addendum No. 2 To O.O. No. 29	08/04/1917	08/04/1917
Miscellaneous	Operations. 1917 Second Phase. Instruction No. 1		
Miscellaneous	Operations. 1917 2nd Phase. Instruction No. 2	21/08/1917	21/08/1917
Operation(al) Order(s)	Operation Order No 30 by Lt K.V. Barred. Comdg. No. 44 M.G. Coy.		
Operation(al) Order(s)	Operation Order No. 31 By Lieut K.V. Barrett Comdg. No 44 M.G. Coy	25/04/1917	25/04/1917
Operation(al) Order(s)	Operation Order No 32 by Lt K.V. Barrett. Comdg. No. 44 M.G. Coy.		
Operation(al) Order(s)	Operation Order No 33 by Lt K.V. Barrett. Comdg. No 44 M.G Coy.		
Heading	Confidential War Diary of The 44th Machine Gun Company From 1st May 1917 to 31st May 1917 (Volume XVI)		
War Diary	Simencourt	01/05/1917	08/05/1917
War Diary	Sombrin	09/05/1917	21/05/1917
War Diary	Fresnoy	22/05/1917	31/05/1917
Operation(al) Order(s)	Operation Order No. 34 by Lieut K.V. Barrett comdg. No. 44 M.G. Coy.		
Operation(al) Order(s)	Operation Order No. 35 by Lieut K.V. Barrett Comdg 44 M.G. Coy 20/5/17	20/05/1917	20/05/1917
Operation(al) Order(s)	Operation Order No. 36 by Lieut K.V. Barrett Comdg 44 M.G. Coy	21/05/1917	21/05/1917
Miscellaneous			
Heading	Confidential War Diary of 44th Machine Gun Coy From 1st June 1917 to 30th June 1917 (Volume XVII)		
War Diary	Fresnoy	01/06/1917	20/06/1917
War Diary	Siracourt	21/06/1917	21/06/1917
War Diary	Antin	22/06/1917	22/06/1917
War Diary	Lespesses	23/06/1917	24/06/1917
War Diary	Thiennes	25/06/1917	25/06/1917
War Diary	Caestre	26/06/1917	26/06/1917
War Diary	Brandhoek	27/06/1917	30/06/1917
Operation(al) Order(s)	Operation Order No. 37 by Capt. K.V. Barrett Commdg 44th M.G. Coy	21/06/1917	21/06/1917

Operation(al) Order(s)	Operation Order No. 38 by Capt. K.V. Barrett Commdg 44 M.G. Coy. 22 June 1917	22/06/1917	22/06/1917
Operation(al) Order(s)	Operation Order No. 39 by Capt K.V. Barrett Commdg 44 M.G. Coy		
Operation(al) Order(s)	Operation Order No. 40 by Capt K.V. Barrett Comdg K.V 44 M.G Coy	25/06/1917	25/06/1917
Operation(al) Order(s)	Operation Order No. 41 by Capt K.V. Barrett Comdg K.V 44 M.G Coy		
Operation(al) Order(s)	Operation Order No. 42 by Capt K.V. Barrett Comdg K.V 44 M.G Coy		
Operation(al) Order(s)	Operation Order No. 43 by Capt K.V. Barrett Comdg 44 M.G. Coy	29/06/1917	29/06/1917
Heading	Confidential War Diary of 44th Machine Gun Coy. From July 1917 to 31st July 1917 Volume XVII (Original)		
War Diary	Toronto Camp Brandhoek	01/07/1917	10/07/1917
War Diary	Robrouck	11/07/1917	17/07/1917
War Diary	Toronto Camp	15/07/1917	19/07/1917
War Diary	Ypres	20/07/1917	22/07/1917
War Diary	Toronto Camp Ypres	23/07/1917	31/07/1917
Miscellaneous	Ypres-1917. Preliminary Instruction by Captain K.V. Barrett Commanding 44th Machine Gun Company		
Map	Battery Positions Trenches Machine Guns Trench Mortars Dumps		
Miscellaneous	Addendum No. 1 Preliminary Instruction Captain K.V. Barrett Cdg 44th Machine Gun Coy		
Miscellaneous	Machine Guns Barrage Preliminary Instruction.		
Miscellaneous	M.G. Fire Organisation Order.		
Operation(al) Order(s)	Operation Order No. 44. by Capt. K.V. Barrett Comdg. 44th M.G. Coy	02/07/1917	02/07/1917
Operation(al) Order(s)	Operation Order No. 45 by Capt K.V. Barrett Comdg. 44th M.G. Coy	08/07/1917	08/07/1917
Operation(al) Order(s)	Operation Order No. 46 by Capt K.V. Barrett Comdg. 44th M.G. Coy	09/07/1917	09/07/1917
Operation(al) Order(s)	Operation Order No. 47 by Capt K.V. Barrett Comdg. 44th M.G. Coy	16/07/1917	16/07/1917
Operation(al) Order(s)	Operation Order No. 49 by Capt K.V. Barrett Comdg. 44th M.G. Coy	22/07/1917	22/07/1917
Operation(al) Order(s)	Operation Order No. 48 by Capt K.V. Barrett Comdg. 44th M.G. Coy	20/07/1917	20/07/1917
Operation(al) Order(s)	Operation Order No. 50 by Capt K.V. Barrett Comdg. 44th M.G. Coy	23/07/1917	23/07/1917
Operation(al) Order(s)	Operation Order No. 51 by Capt K.V. Barrett Comdg. 44th M.G. Coy		
Miscellaneous	A Form Messages And Signals.		
Miscellaneous	O.C. 52		
Miscellaneous	A Form. Messages And Signals.		
Operation(al) Order(s)	Operation Order No. 52 by Captain V. Barrett Cmdg. 44 M.G. Coy.	20/07/1917	20/07/1917
Miscellaneous	A Form Messages And Signals.		
Operation(al) Order(s)	Operation Order No. 53. by Capt. K.V. Barrett Comdg 44 M.G. Coy	28/07/1917	28/07/1917
Operation(al) Order(s)	Operations Order No. 54. By Capt. K.V. Barrett Comdg. 44th M.G. Coty.	30/07/1917	30/07/1917

Heading	Confidential War Diary of 44th Machine Gun Company from August 1st 1917 to August 31st 1917 Volume XIX		
War Diary	Ypres	01/08/1917	03/08/1917
War Diary	Winnezeele	04/08/1917	17/08/1917
War Diary	Poperinghe	18/08/1917	19/08/1917
War Diary	Ypres	02/08/1917	31/08/1917
Miscellaneous	Preliminary Instruction by Lieut E Rogers Comdg 44th M.G. Coy 20 August 1917	20/08/1917	20/08/1917
Operation(al) Order(s)	Operation Order No. 53 by Lt Colonel Rogers Commdg. No 44 M.G. Coy	19/08/1917	19/08/1917
Operation(al) Order(s)	Operation Order No. 57. By Lieut E. Rogers. Commdg. M.G. Coy	17/08/1917	17/08/1917
Heading	Confidential (Original) War Diary of 44th Coy Machine Gun Corps. From 1st Sept 1917 to 30th Sept 1917 Volume XX		
War Diary	Lens 3H 53.68	01/09/1917	05/09/1917
War Diary	C 18.C, 1.9 51 B N.W.	06/09/1917	30/09/1917
Operation(al) Order(s)	Operation Order No. 54 by Capt K.V. Barrett Comdg 44th M.G. Coy	14/09/1917	14/09/1917
Heading	Confidential War Diary of 44th Machine Gun Company from 1st October 1917 to 31st October 1917 (Volume XXI)		
War Diary	Dingwall Camp	01/10/1917	12/10/1917
War Diary	Arras	14/10/1917	31/10/1917
Operation(al) Order(s)	Operation Order No. 55 By Capt K.V. Barrett Comdg 44 M.G. Coy	08/10/1917	08/10/1917
Operation(al) Order(s)	Operation Order No. 56 by Capt K.V. Barrett. H.C. Comdg 44th M.G. Coy 24th October 1917	24/10/1917	24/10/1917
Heading	Confidential War Diary For Month of November 1917 of 44th Machine Gun Company Volume XXII		
War Diary	Arras	01/11/1917	01/11/1917
War Diary	Field	02/11/1917	18/11/1917
War Diary	Arras	19/11/1917	25/11/1917
War Diary	Field	26/11/1917	28/11/1917
War Diary	Arras	29/11/1917	30/11/1917
Heading	War Diary of Machine Gun Coy for December 1917 Volume XXIII		
War Diary		01/12/1917	31/12/1917
Heading	Confidential War Diary of 44th M.G. Coy From 1st Jan. 1918 To 31st Jan 1918 Volume XXIV		
War Diary		01/01/1918	31/01/1918
Miscellaneous		01/01/1918	01/01/1918
Operation(al) Order(s)	Operation Order No.1 By Capt K.V. Barrett M.G. Comdg 44th Machine Gun Company		
Operation(al) Order(s)	Operation Order No. 65 by Lieut Roqin Comdg MG Coy		
Heading	Confidential War Diary of 44th Machine Gun Company A Coy. 15th Batt M.G.C. From 1st February 1918 to 28th February Vol XXV		
War Diary		01/02/1918	28/02/1918
Operation(al) Order(s)	Operation Order No. 64 by Lieut E Rogers Comdg 44 M.G. Coy		
Miscellaneous	Addendum No. 1 T 44 M.G. Coy O.O. 64		
Operation(al) Order(s)	Operation Order No. 66 By Lieut E. Rogers. Comdg 44th M.G. Coy.		

Operation(al) Order(s)	Operation Order No. 66 By Lieut E. Rogers. Comdg 44th M.G. Coy	21/02/1918	21/02/1918
Operation(al) Order(s)	Operation Order No. 67 By Lieut E. Rogers. Comdg 44th M.G. Coy	21/02/1918	21/02/1918

WO95 1941/2

1916 Mar - 1918 Feb

No 44 Brigade Machine Gun Company

15TH DIVISION
44TH INFY BDE

44TH MACHINE GUN COY.

MAR 1916 - FEB 1918

Instructions regarding War Diaries and Intelligence Summaries are contained in F. S. Regs., Part II. and the Staff Manual respectively. Title Pages will be prepared in manuscript.

WAR DIARY
or
INTELLIGENCE SUMMARY
(Erase heading not required.)

Army Form C. 2118

Place	Date	Hour	Summary of Events and Information	Remarks and references to Appendices
			No 44 Brigade Machine Gun Company WAR DIARY for the month of March 1916. Feb '18	44 M G C Vol 1

1875 Wt. W593/826 1,000,000 4/15 J.B.C. & A. A.D.S.S./Forms/C. 2118.

Army Form C. 2118

Instructions regarding War Diaries and Intelligence Summaries are contained in F. S. Regs., Part II. and the Staff Manual respectively. Title Pages will be prepared in manuscript.

WAR DIARY
or
~~INTELLIGENCE SUMMARY~~
(Erase heading not required.)

Place	Date	Hour	Summary of Events and Information	Remarks and references to Appendices
Mazingarbe	1916 1st Mar.		No. 46 Company relieved No 44 Machine Gun Company in trenches in the Loos Sector.	
do.	2nd Mar.		Left ~~Gosnay~~ Mazingarbe and proceeded to Gosnay, near Béthune, for 6 days' rest.	
Gosnay	3rd Mar.		No training could be done owing to bad weather.	
do	4th Mar.		Very bad weather interfered with training	
do	5th Mar.		Firing on range. Motor Machine Gun School. Also night firing. 2/Lt. A. J. Wright returned to England for Munition Work.	
do	6th Mar.		Nothing to report.	
do	7th Mar.		No 44 Company relieved No 46 Machine Gun Company in trenches in the Hulloch Sector	
Mazingarbe	8th Mar.		Nothing to report	
do	9th Mar.		Nothing to report	
do	10th Mar.		Fire opened on enemy's Ration "dump". Effect could not be seen	

1875 Wt. W593/826 1,000,000 4/15 J.B.C. & A. A.D.S.S./Forms/C. 2118.

Army Form C. 2118

Instructions regarding War Diaries and Intelligence Summaries are contained in F. S. Regs., Part II. and the Staff Manual respectively. Title Pages will be prepared in manuscript.

WAR DIARY
~~or~~
~~INTELLIGENCE SUMMARY~~

(Erase heading not required.)

Place	Date	Hour	Summary of Events and Information	Remarks and references to Appendices
Mazingarbe.	1916 11th Mar.		Nothing to report.	
do	12th Mar.		Gun No C. 10 fired on and dispersed enemy bombing party.	
do	13th Mar.		First Company relief.	
do.	14th Mar.		"C" Section relieved by 7th Camerons.	
do	15th Mar.		Nothing to report.	
do.	16th Mar.		Nothing to report.	
do	17th Mar.		Nothing to report	
do.	18th Mar.		Enemy exploded mine. Our guns opened rapid fire. No Infantry attack	
do.	19th Mar.		No. 46 Company relieved No. 44 Machine Gun Company in trenches in the Hulloch Sector moved into billets at Noeux-les-Mines.	
Noeux-les-Mines	20th Mar.		Bad weather interfered with training	

1875 Wt. W593/826 1,000,000 4/15 J.B.C. & A. A.D.S.S./Forms/C. 2118.

Army Form C. 2118

Instructions regarding War Diaries and Intelligence Summaries are contained in F. S. Regs., Part II. and the Staff Manual respectively. Title Pages will be prepared in manuscript.

WAR DIARY

~~or~~

~~INTELLIGENCE SUMMARY~~

(Erase heading not required.)

Place	Date	Hour	Summary of Events and Information	Remarks and references to Appendices
Noeux-les-Mines	1916 21st Mar.		Training proceeded with	
do.	22nd Mar.		Training proceeded with	
do.	23rd Mar.		Training prevented owing to bad weather	
do.	24th Mar.		No. 44 Company relieved No. 45 Machine Gun Company in trenches in Loos Sector.	
Mazingarbe	25th Mar.		Nothing to report.	
do	26th Mar.		Nothing to report.	
do	27th Mar.		Nothing to report.	
do	28th Mar.		Nothing to report.	
do	29th Mar.		Nothing to report.	
do	30th Mar.		Nothing to report	
do	31st Mar.		Nothing to report	

[signature] Captain
Cmdg. No. 44 M. G. Coy.

1875 Wt. W593/826 1,000,000 4/15 J.B.C. & A. A.D.S.S./Forms/C. 2118.

Instructions regarding War Diaries and Intelligence Summaries are contained in F. S. Regs., Part II. and the Staff Manual respectively. Title Pages will be prepared in manuscript.

WAR DIARY
or
INTELLIGENCE SUMMARY
(Erase heading not required.)

XV

Army Form C. 2118

44 M G Coy

Vol 2

Place	Date	Hour	Summary of Events and Information	Remarks and references to Appendices
			No 44 Machine Gun Coy WAR DIARY Month of April 1916. [signature] Captain Cmdg. No 44 M.G. Coy.	

1875 Wt. W593/826 1,000,000 4/15 J.B.C. & A. A.D.S.S./Forms/C. 2118.

Army Form C. 2118

Instructions regarding War Diaries and Intelligence Summaries are contained in F. S. Regs., Part II. and the Staff Manual respectively. Title Pages will be prepared in manuscript.

WAR DIARY
or
~~INTELLIGENCE SUMMARY~~

(Erase heading not required.)

Place	Date	Hour	Summary of Events and Information	Remarks and references to Appendices
Mazingarbe	1916. Apr 1st		46 M. G. Coy relieved this company in trenches. ~~Loos Sector~~ 14 Bis Sector.	
Allouagne	2nd		Company moved to Allouagne to join 15th Division at rest.	
do.	3rd		Devoted to cleaning limbers, guns, equipment, etc.	
do.	4th		Nothing to report	
do.	5th		Training proceeded with.	
do.	6th		Training proceeded with.	
do.	7th		Company moved with Brigade to Febvin Palfart on Divisional Tactical March.	
Febvin Palfart	8th		Brigade Operations.	
Allouagne	9th		Company returned with Brigade to Allouagne.	
do.	10th		Smoke demonstration at Rainbert.	

1375 Wt. W593/826 1,000,000 4/15 J.B.C. & A. A.D.S.S./Forms/C. 2118.

Army Form C. 2118

Instructions regarding War Diaries and Intelligence Summaries are contained in F. S. Regs., Part II. and the Staff Manual respectively. Title Pages will be prepared in manuscript.

WAR DIARY

~~or~~

~~INTELLIGENCE SUMMARY~~

(Erase heading not required.)

Place	Date	Hour	Summary of Events and Information	Remarks and references to Appendices
Allouagne	1916. April. 11th		Training proceeded with.	
do.	12th		Firing on the range.	
do.	13th		Firing on the range.	
do.	14th		Firing on the range. Other training proceeded with.	
do.	15th		Training proceeded with.	
do.	16th	11.45 a.m.	Company attended Church Parade.	
do.	17th		Nothing to report.	
do.	18th		Training carried out.	
do.	19th		Training carried out.	
do	20th		Firing on the range.	

1875 Wt. W593/826 1,000,000 4/15 J.B.C. & A. A.D.S.S./Forms/C. 2118.

Army Form C. 2118

Instructions regarding War Diaries and Intelligence Summaries are contained in F. S. Regs., Part II. and the Staff Manual respectively. Title Pages will be prepared in manuscript.

WAR DIARY
~~or~~
~~INTELLIGENCE SUMMARY~~
(Erase heading not required.)

Place	Date	Hour	Summary of Events and Information	Remarks and references to Appendices
Allouagne.	1916 April. 21st.		Firing on the range.	
	22nd		Firing on the range.	
	23rd	11.45 a.m.	Company attended Church Parade.	
	24th.		Training proceeded with.	
	25th.		Company moved to Noyelles. 15 Guns relieved guns of No. 36 M.G. Coy in Quarries Sector.	
	26th.		Nothing to report.	
	27th.		Hostile Gas Attack with "Tear" and Asphyxiating Shells. 2 Guns of this Company fired in support of defence of Crater.	
	28th.		Gas alarm received at 9.15 p.m. Company "stood to" until 10.30 p.m.	
	29th.		1 Gun team under Cpl. Smith of D Section was surprised by Gas Attack. Gun opened fire and fired 1800 rounds. The entire team suffered from gas poisoning. Corpl. Smith and two men died the same morning.	
	30th.		Our Guns supported bombing attack.	

1875 Wt. W593/826 1,000,000 4/15 J.B.C. & A. A.D.S.S./Forms/C. 2118.

44 M G Coy
Vol 3

XV

Army Form C. 2118.

Instructions regarding War Diaries and Intelligence Summaries are contained in F. S. Regs., Part II. and the Staff Manual respectively. Title Pages will be prepared in manuscript.

WAR DIARY
or
INTELLIGENCE SUMMARY
(Erase heading not required.)

Place	Date	Hour	Summary of Events and Information	Remarks and references to Appendices
			WAR DIARY for the month of May 1916. [signature] Captain, Cmdg. No 44 MACHINE GUN COMPANY.	

1875 Wt. W593/826 1,000,000 4/15 J.B.C. & A. A.D.S.S./Forms/C. 2118.

Army Form C. 2118

Instructions regarding War Diaries and Intelligence Summaries are contained in F. S. Regs., Part II. and the Staff Manual respectively. Title Pages will be prepared in manuscript.

WAR DIARY
~~or~~
~~INTELLIGENCE SUMMARY~~

(Erase heading not required.)

Place	Date	Hour	Summary of Events and Information	Remarks and references to Appendices
Noyelles.	1st May		Nothing to report.	
do.	2nd May		Nothing to report.	
do.	3rd May		Gas alarm received 2.48 a.m. (False Alarm).	
do.	4th May		Nothing to report.	
do.	5th May		Situation normal. Nothing to report.	
do.	6th May		1000 rounds fired at enemy ration dump and 1000 rounds at cross roads where enemy transport passes.	
do.	7th May		Nothing to report.	
do	8th May		Situation unchanged. Nothing to report.	
do.	9th May		Nothing to report.	
do.	10th May		No. 46 M. G. Coy. relieved Company in Quarries Sector. Company moved to Béthune for 8 days rest.	

1875 Wt. W593/826 1,000,000 4/15 J.B.C. & A. A.D.S.S./Forms/C. 2118.

Instructions regarding War Diaries and Intelligence Summaries are contained in F. S. Regs., Part II. and the Staff Manual respectively. Title Pages will be prepared in manuscript.

WAR DIARY

~~or~~

~~INTELLIGENCE SUMMARY~~

(Erase heading not required.)

Army Form C. 2118

Place	Date	Hour	Summary of Events and Information	Remarks and references to Appendices
Béthune.	11th May.	5 p.m.	Company ordered to "stand to" ready to move at half-an-hour's notice.	
do.	12th May		Nothing to report.	
do.	13th May.		Order to be ready to move cancelled.	
do.	14th May		Company ordered to "stand to" ready to move at one hour's notice.	
do.	15th May		Nothing to report.	
do.	16th May		Nothing to report.	
do.	17th May		Nothing to report.	
do.	18th May		This Company relieved No. 46 M. G. Coy. in Hohenzollern Sector. Company Headquarters moved to Brewery, VERMELLES.	
Vermelles.	19th May		Nothing to report.	
do.	20th May		Situation unchanged.	

1875 Wt. W593/826 1,000,000 4/15 J.B.C. & A. A.D.S.S./Forms/C. 2118.

Instructions regarding War Diaries and Intelligence Summaries are contained in F. S. Regs., Part II. and the Staff Manual respectively. Title Pages will be prepared in manuscript.

WAR DIARY

~~or~~

~~INTELLIGENCE SUMMARY~~

(Erase heading not required.)

Army Form C. 2118

Place	Date	Hour	Summary of Events and Information	Remarks and references to Appendices
Vermelles	21st May		Several lachrymatory shells fell in the vicinity of Vermelles	
do	22nd May		1500 rounds fired on enemy communication trenches.	
do.	23rd May		Nothing to report.	
do.	24th May		1500 rounds fired on enemy communication trenches.	
do.	25th May	9.30pm	1000 rounds fired on enemy communication trenches.	
do.	26th May		5000 rounds fired on roads behind enemy lines.	
do.	27th May		Situation normal. Nothing to report.	
do	28th May		4750 rounds fired on HAISNES - DOUVAIN road.	
do.	29th May		5000 rounds fired on roads behind enemy lines.	
do.	30th May		Nothing to report.	
do.	31st May		Situation normal. Nothing to report.	

1875 Wt. W593/826 1,000,000 4/15 J.B.C. & A. A.D.S.S./Forms/C. 2118.

XV

Instructions regarding War Diaries and Intelligence Summaries are contained in F. S. Regs., Part II. and the Staff Manual respectively. Title Pages will be prepared in manuscript.

WAR DIARY
or
INTELLIGENCE SUMMARY
(Erase heading not required.)

Army Form C. 2118

44 M G Coy
Vol 4

Place	Date	Hour	Summary of Events and Information	Remarks and references to Appendices

No 44 BDE. M. G. COY.

WAR DIARY.

for the month of JUNE 1916.

VOLUME 5

Confidential

[signature] Captain,
Cmdg. No 44 M.G. Coy.

1875 Wt. W593/826 1,000,000 4/15 J.B.C. & A. A.D.S.S./Forms/C. 2118.

Instructions regarding War Diaries and Intelligence Summaries are contained in F. S. Regs., Part II. and the Staff Manual respectively. Title Pages will be prepared in manuscript.

WAR DIARY

~~or~~

~~INTELLIGENCE SUMMARY~~

(Erase heading not required.)

Army Form C. 2118

Place	Date	Hour	Summary of Events and Information	Remarks and references to Appendices
Vermelles.	1916 June 1st		Nothing to report.	
do.	2nd		Situation unchanged.	
do.	3rd		No 46 Coy. relieved this Company in Hohenzollern Section. This Company moved to NOYELLES, but left 5 guns in VILLAGE LINE.	
Noyelles.	4th		Nothing to report. News of Naval Battle off Jutland received.	
do.	5th		Guns in VILLAGE LINE relieved.	
do	6th		Nothing to report.	
do.	7th		Situation normal. News received of Lord Kitchener's death	
do.	8th		Guns in VILLAGE LINE relieved.	
do.	9th		Nothing to report	
do.	10th		Situation normal. Nothing to report.	
do	11th		This Company relieved No 45 Coy. in Hulluch Section. Guns in VILLAGE LINE relieved by No 45 Coy.	
		6.30 pm.	100 rounds fired at enemy working party and dispersed same.	
do	12th		Nothing to report	
do.	13th	11 p.m	500 rounds fired on enemy's communication trenches	

Instructions regarding War Diaries and Intelligence Summaries are contained in F. S. Regs., Part II. and the Staff Manual respectively. Title Pages will be prepared in manuscript.

WAR DIARY

~~or~~

~~INTELLIGENCE SUMMARY~~

(Erase heading not required.)

Army Form C. 2118

Place	Date	Hour	Summary of Events and Information	Remarks and references to Appendices
Noyelles	1916 June 14th		Nothing to report	
do	15th		Nothing to report. Situation normal	
do	16th	12 midnt to 1 a.m.	1000 rounds fired at tracks behind CITÉ ST. ELIE.	
do	17th	12 midnight	500 rounds fired at tracks in CITÉ ST. ELIE.	
do.	18th	11.0 to 11.45 p.m.	1000 rounds fired on enemy's communication trenches.	
do.	19th		Nothing to report.	
do	20th	11 p.m. to 1 a.m.	2000 rounds fired on enemy's communication trenches.	
do.	21st		Nothing to report. Situation normal.	
do.	22nd	11.30 p.m. to 12.15 a.m.	2000 rounds fired on enemy's communication trenches. near CITE ST. ELIE.	
do.	23rd		Situation unchanged. Nothing to report.	
do.	24th		10,000 rounds were fired on enemy communication trenches at 11 p.m. and 2 a.m. for 8 ~~[illegible]~~ minutes at at time. Eight guns were used and the enemy communication trenches and roads were searched for ranges between 2000 and 2800 yards.	

1875 Wt. W593/826 1,000,000 4/15 J.B.C. & A. A.D.S.S./Forms/C. 2118.

Army Form C. 2118

Instructions regarding War Diaries and Intelligence Summaries are contained in F. S. Regs., Part II. and the Staff Manual respectively. Title Pages will be prepared in manuscript.

WAR DIARY

or

~~INTELLIGENCE SUMMARY~~

(Erase heading not required.)

Place	Date	Hour	Summary of Events and Information	Remarks and references to Appendices
Noyelles	1916 June 25th		7000 rounds fired on enemy communication trenches, roads, dumps and tramways between 12·55 and 1·5 a.m. Eight guns were used for indirect fire. Machine guns were also fired to keep gaps in enemy's wire opened. Between 1·30 a.m. and 2·30 a.m. 2000 rounds from aeroplane mountings.	
do.	26th		19000 rounds fired on enemy's communication trenches, roads, dumps and tramways between 11 p.m. and 1·4 a.m. Ranges from 2000 to 2800 – 10 guns used. Between 2 a.m and 4 a.m. 5000 rounds were fired at aeroplanes from aerial mountings.	
do.	27th		No. 46 Coy. relieved this Coy. in the Hulluch Section. 5 guns were taken over in the VILLAGE LINE, remainder of Company resting in Noyelles.	
do.	28th		Devoted to cleaning guns, limbers, equipment etc.	
do	29th		Nothing to report.	
do.	30th		Nothing to report	

1875 Wt. W593/826 1,000,000 4/15 J.B.C. & A. A.D.S.S./Forms/C. 2118.

15 July
44 MGC
Vol 5

Army Form C. 2118.

Instructions regarding War Diaries and Intelligence Summaries are contained in F. S. Regs., Part II. and the Staff Manual respectively. Title Pages will be prepared in manuscript.

WAR DIARY
or
~~INTELLIGENCE SUMMARY~~
(Erase heading not required.)

Place	Date	Hour	Summary of Events and Information	Remarks and references to Appendices
			No. 44 MACHINE GUN COMPANY.	
			WAR DIARY.	
			for the month of JULY 1916. —	
			[signature] Captain Commanding No. 44 M. G. Coy.	

1875 Wt. W593/826 1,000,000 4/15 J.B.C. & A. A.D.S.S./Forms/C. 2118.

To/
Headquarters
44th Infantry Bde

Herewith War Diary of No 44 Machine Gun Company for the month of July 1916.

Delay regretted.

[signature]
Captain
Cmdg No 44 M. G. Coy

1-8-1916

Army Form C. 2118

Instructions regarding War Diaries and Intelligence Summaries are contained in F. S. Regs., Part II. and the Staff Manual respectively. Title Pages will be prepared in manuscript.

WAR DIARY
or
~~INTELLIGENCE SUMMARY~~

(Erase heading not required.)

Place	Date	Hour	Summary of Events and Information	Remarks and references to Appendices
NOYELLES.	1916 July 1st		5 guns in the VILLAGE LINE relieved. Instruction in Machine Gun work proceeded with by remainder of Company at rest.	
do	2nd		Company attended Church Parade at the Château, NOYELLES.	
do.	3rd		Training proceeded with. N. C. O's fired at night to test new type of stove pipe attachment which was found useless. 8 guns sent to Divisional Workshop to be overhauled.	
do.	4th		Instruction in Machine Gun work proceeded with. Remaining 8 guns sent for overhauling.	
do VERMELLES.	5th		12 guns of this Coy. (3 from each Section) relieved 45 M. G. Coy. in the HOHENZOLLERN SECTION. Relief completed at 3.p.m. The guns occupied positions as follows: 7 in Reserve Line and 5 in Village Line. Between 11.25 and 11.35 p.m. 1500 rounds fired on enemy's communication trenches, and tracks in CITÉ ST. ELIE. General improvements carried out at all positions.	
do	6th	3 p.m.	2/Lt. A. J. Rayner died from gun shot wound in the head, at his Section's emplacement in the Reserve Line. No indirect fire could be carried out owing to working parties.	

1875 Wt. W593/826 1,000,000 4/15 J.B.C. & A. A.D.S.S./Forms/C. 2118.

Army Form C. 2118

WAR DIARY

or

~~INTELLIGENCE SUMMARY~~

(Erase heading not required.)

Instructions regarding War Diaries and Intelligence Summaries are contained in F. S. Regs., Part II. and the Staff Manual respectively. Title Pages will be prepared in manuscript.

Place	Date	Hour	Summary of Events and Information	Remarks and references to Appendices
VERMELLES.	1916 July 7th		8000 rounds were fired indirectly on enemy's trenches, tramway's etc, between 11·30 p.m. and 12·15 a.m.	
do.	8th		6000 rounds fired between 12 midnight and 1·15 a.m. on enemy's communication trenches.	
do.	9th		5000 rounds were fired indirectly between 11·15 and 11·30 p.m. on enemy's trenches. When firing ceased, enemy's artillery retaliated with shrapnel and small H.E. Shells.	
do.	10th		At 8-20 a.m. telephone message was received to the effect that hostile working party were at work near enemy's reserve line. 250 rounds were fired indirectly, but result could not be ascertained. 7500 rounds were fired in support of raid carried out by 8th Seaforth Hdrs.	
do	11th		4500 rounds fired on enemy's trenches, light railways, roads etc, between 10·45 and 11·50 p.m.	
do	12th		4500 rounds fired between 11·15 and 11·50 p.m. on enemy's roads, light railways and communication trenches	
do	13th		Indirect fire carried out between 11 and 11·30 p.m, and between 2 and 3·30 a.m, 6500 rounds being fired on enemy's communication trenches, roads etc.	

1875 Wt. W593/826 1,000,000 4/15 J.B.C. & A. A.D.S.S./Forms/C. 2118.

Instructions regarding War Diaries and Intelligence Summaries are contained in F. S. Regs., Part II. and the Staff Manual respectively. Title Pages will be prepared in manuscript.

WAR DIARY

~~or~~

~~INTELLIGENCE SUMMARY~~

(Erase heading not required.)

Army Form C. 2118

Place	Date	Hour	Summary of Events and Information	Remarks and references to Appendices
VERMELLES.	1916 July 14th		9000 rounds were fired between 10·30 and 11 p.m., and between 12·15 and 12·45 a.m. on enemy's trenches, light railways, roads, etc.	
do	15th		6000 rounds on enemy's communication trenches between 1 a.m. and 1·45 a.m.	
do	16th		7000 rounds on enemy's roads near CITÉ ST. ELIE between 11·30 p.m. and 12·20 a.m.	
do	17th		6000 rounds fired on enemy's communication trenches.	
do	18th		6000 rounds fired indirectly on enemy's trenches and roads between 12·15 p.m. and 1 a.m.	
do	19th		9000 rounds fired on enemy's trenches and light railways between 1 and 2 a.m.	
do	20th		~~Nothing to report~~ 6000 rounds fired on enemy's communication trenches.	
do	21st		No. 25 M. G. Coy. relieved this Coy. in the HOHENZOLLERN SECTOR. Relief completed at 4 p.m.	
do	22nd		This Coy. moved to NOEUX-LES-MINES.	

1875 Wt. W593/826 1,000,000 4/15 J.B.C. & A. A.D.S.S./Forms/C. 2118.

Instructions regarding War Diaries and Intelligence Summaries are contained in F. S. Regs., Part II. and the Staff Manual respectively. Title Pages will be prepared in manuscript.

WAR DIARY

~~or~~

~~INTELLIGENCE SUMMARY~~

(Erase heading not required.)

Army Form C. 2118

Place	Date	Hour	Summary of Events and Information	Remarks and references to Appendices
NOEUX LES MINES	1916 July 23rd	8.30 a.m.	Company moved with Brigade to LA THIEULOYE, via BRUAY. Arrived at 4 p.m.	
LA THIEULOYE	24th		Day devoted to cleaning limbers, guns etc. and re-equipment of men.	
do	25th		Training in wood fighting carried out. 7 Other Ranks joined Company as reinforcements.	
do	26th	7 a.m.	Company moved off to AVERDOINGT arriving at 10.15 a.m.	
AVERDOINGT	27th	6 a.m.	Company marched with Brigade to REMAISNIL	
REMAISNIL	28th	6.30 a.m.	Company moved to GÉZAINECOURT. with Brigade.	
GÉZAINECOURT	29th		Training carried out.	
do	30th	11.0 a.m.	Company attended Church Parade.	
do.	31st	3-0 a.m.	Company march to WARGNIES via NAOURS.	

1875 Wt. W593/826 1,000,000 4/15 J.B.C. & A. A.D.S.S./Forms/C. 2118.

44th Brigade.

15th Division.

44th BRIGADE MACHINE GUN COMPANY

AUGUST 1 9 1 6

Army Form C. 2118

15

44 MGC

Vol 6

Instructions regarding War Diaries and Intelligence Summaries are contained in F. S. Regs., Part II. and the Staff Manual respectively. Title Pages will be prepared in manuscript.

WAR DIARY
or
INTELLIGENCE SUMMARY
(Erase heading not required.)

Place	Date	Hour	Summary of Events and Information	Remarks and references to Appendices
			No. 44 Machine Gun Coy.	
			WAR DIARY	
			for the month of AUGUST 1916.	
			[signature] Captain Commanding No. 44 M. G. Coy	

1875 Wt. W593/826 1,000,000 4/15 J.B.C. & A. A.D.S.S./Forms/C. 2118.

Army Form C. 2118

Instructions regarding War Diaries and Intelligence Summaries are contained in F. S. Regs., Part II. and the Staff Manual respectively. Title Pages will be prepared in manuscript.

WAR DIARY

or

~~INTELLIGENCE SUMMARY~~

(Erase heading not required.)

Place	Date	Hour	Summary of Events and Information	Remarks and references to Appendices
WARGNIES.	1st 2nd & 3rd		In billets at WARGNIES. Training in tactical handling of machine guns, and in wood fighting was carried out.	
do.	4th	4-15 a.m. 8-15 am	Coy. moved off with Brigade to MIRVAUX arriving at 8 am. Billeting completed.	
MIRVAUX	5th	7.15 a.m. 10.10 am	Coy. marched with Brigade to BÉHENCOURT arriving at 9.55 am. Billeting completed.	
BÉHENCOURT.	6th	11.15 am.	Company attended Church Parade at BÉHENCOURT.	
do.	7th		Devoted to cleaning and packing up.	
do.	8th	1 a.m. 7 am	Coy. left BÉHENCOURT and marched to ALBERT. No. 68 M. G. Coy. was relieved in Divisional Reserve in bivouac at pt. W. 3. d. 1. 9. approx. Relief complete	
ALBERT	9th 10th 11th		Training in Machine Gun work carried out	

1875 Wt. W593/826 1,000,000 4/15 J.B.C. & A. A.D.S.S./Forms/C. 2118.

Army Form C. 2118

Instructions regarding War Diaries and Intelligence Summaries are contained in F. S. Regs., Part II. and the Staff Manual respectively. Title Pages will be prepared in manuscript.

WAR DIARY

or

~~INTELLIGENCE SUMMARY~~

(Erase heading not required.)

Place	Date	Hour	Summary of Events and Information	Remarks and references to Appendices
ALBERT	12th	6.30 p.m. 8.10 "	Coy. moved up to pt. E.5.b.7.7. in bivouac vacated by 9th Black Watch. Movement completed. All transport, except fighting limbers, left in the transport lines W. of ALBERT	
do.	13th	 10 p.m.	Coy. relieved No. 45 M. G. Coy. Relief complete. 9 guns taken over in front line system + 2 in support at CONTALMAISON. Transport and Q.M. Stores left in BÉCOURT WOOD 2000 rds. were fired during night and early morning at parties of enemy. Men were seen to fall and parties were dispersed. 500 rds. used in sniping with Machine Guns during morning at small parties of enemy moving out of shell holes. Casualties were inflicted. Own casualties. Killed 1 Cpl. Wounded. 1 man	
CONTALMAISON	14th	 8 to 9 a.m.	1000 rds used in sniping with Machine Guns parties of enemy near roads and shell holes during night and early morning. 1500 rds. fired at parties seen 700 yards N.W. of MARTINPUICH advancing in open order across green fields. Parties dispersed and casualties inflicted. 1000 rds used in indirect fire on E. end of MARTINPUICH. Own casualties. 2 men Wounded.	

1875 Wt. W593/826 1,000,000 4/15 J.B.C. & A. A.D.S.S./Forms/C. 2118.

Instructions regarding War Diaries and Intelligence Summaries are contained in F. S. Regs., Part II. and the Staff Manual respectively. Title Pages will be prepared in manuscript.

WAR DIARY
or
~~INTELLIGENCE SUMMARY~~
(Erase heading not required.)

Army Form C. 2118

Place	Date	Hour	Summary of Events and Information	Remarks and references to Appendices
CONTALMAISON	15th		1000 rds. fired at small parties of enemy in shell holes during morning. 1000 rds. used in Indirect fire on Eastern end of MARTINPUICH. 500 rds fired at enemy aeroplane which was driven back. Own casualties. 2 men wounded	
do.	16th		5000 rds fired at enemy on flank and on communication trench. Enemy were observed to fall disperse. 3500 rds. fired at enemy bombers and retiring infantry. Large casualties claimed. Own casualties. 2 men wounded	
do	17th		Capture of German SWITCH TRENCH. In order to assist the operation guns were moved to positions marked on enclosed map. The gun at A could bring oblique fire to bear on the ~~point~~ ground behind the point attacked. The one at B could deal with ground S. and W. of MARTINPUICH. The gun at C protected left flank from snipers who could approach to within 300 yards under cover. The one at D covered the right flank of the attack. As soon as our infantry went over, the gun at A opened fire and dispersed bombers who moved out of shell holes on the left of the attacking party. About ½ hour after the bombardment started the guns at A + B fired on small parties of enemy attempting to escape in rear and to the left of the area attacked. The gun at C fired on an enemy party bringing up a machine gun. The enemy gun was withdrawn. About midday the enemy bombarded the trench in which A, B, & C. were situated. Guns at B & C were buried, and both teams with the single exception of one carrier, were wiped out.	Map attached.

1875 Wt. W593/826 1,000,000 4/15 J.B.C. & A. A.D.S.S./Forms/C. 2118.

Army Form C. 2118

Instructions regarding War Diaries and Intelligence Summaries are contained in F. S. Regs., Part II. and the Staff Manual respectively. Title Pages will be prepared in manuscript.

WAR DIARY
or
~~INTELLIGENCE SUMMARY~~

(Erase heading not required.)

Place	Date	Hour	Summary of Events and Information	Remarks and references to Appendices
CONTALMAISON	17th (contd)		In spite of the bombardment, the team of A gun was distributed among the 3 guns, and the 2 buried guns were dug out out and brought into action. During the afternoon several parties about 20 strong were seen advancing in ~~the~~ line down slope S.W. of MARTINPUICH. These parties were dispersed. The gun at D opened fire at parties of from 2 to 6. Some men were seen to fall.	
do.	18th		750 rounds fired in support of attack by Australians on our left. Severe bombardment by enemy resulted in 2 guns being buried, one of which was put out of action. Casualties through the bombardment were heavy. 1 Officer wounded (2/Lt A.V.L. Hadaway), O. Rks 5 Killed and 22 wounded.	
do.	19th		500 rounds fired at enemy aeroplanes	
do.	20th 21st 22nd		Nothing to report.	
do.	23rd		1250 rounds fired at enemy aeroplanes.	
do.	24th 25th 26th		Nothing to report.	

1875 Wt. W593/826 1,000,000 4/15 J.B.C. & A. A.D.S.S./Forms/C. 2118.

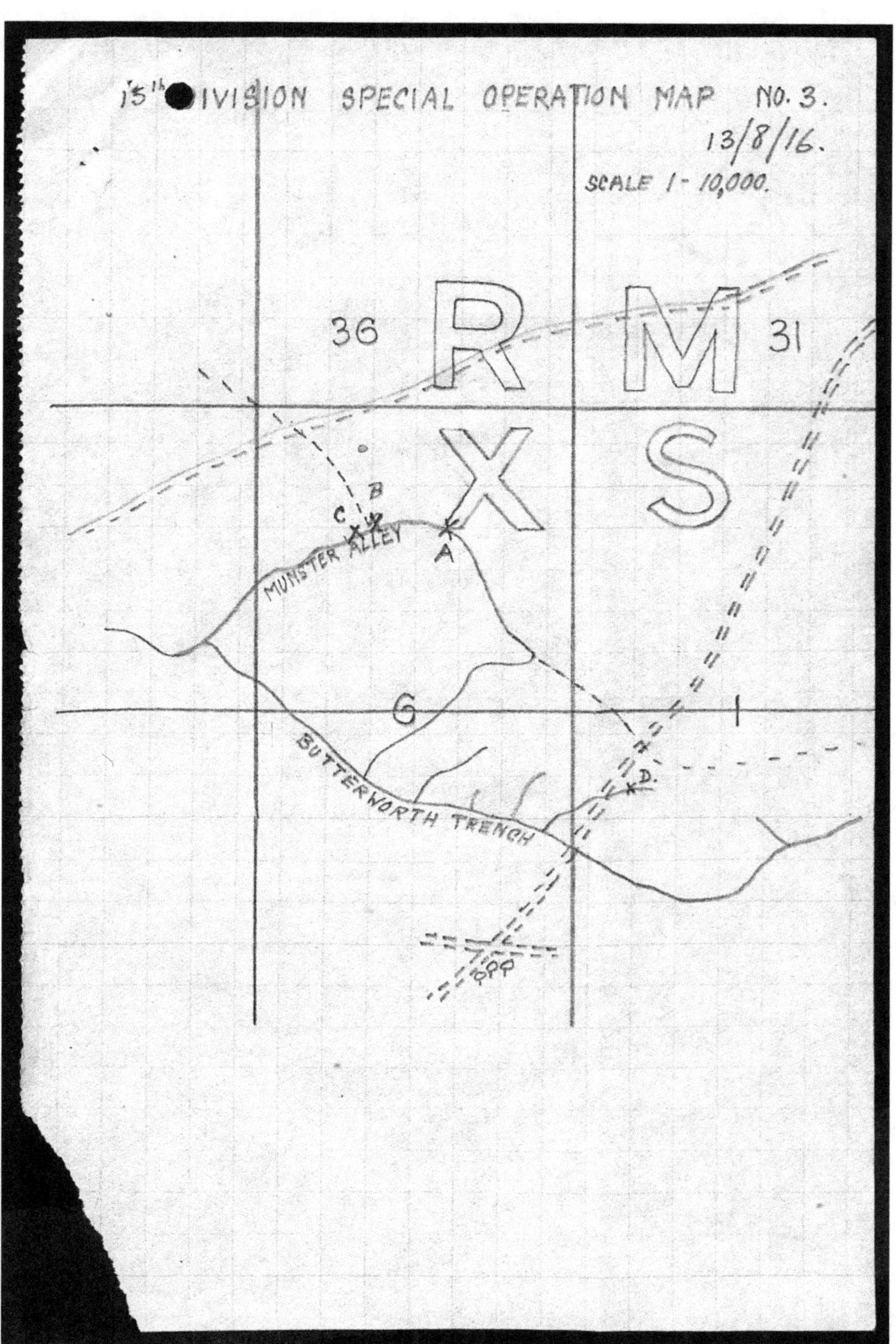
15th DIVISION SPECIAL OPERATION MAP NO. 3.
13/8/16.
SCALE 1-10,000.
R
M
36
31
X
S
B
C
A
MUNSTER ALLEY
6
1
BUTTERWORTH TRENCH
D.

Army Form C. 2118

Instructions regarding War Diaries and Intelligence Summaries are contained in F. S. Regs., Part II. and the Staff Manual respectively. Title Pages will be prepared in manuscript.

WAR DIARY

or

~~INTELLIGENCE SUMMARY~~

(Erase heading not required.)

Place	Date	Hour	Summary of Events and Information	Remarks and references to Appendices
CONTALMAISON	27th		8000 rounds fired between 8-30 p.m. and 1-15 a.m. on enemy roads, tracks and communication trenches near MARTINPUICH.	
do.	28th		9000 rounds fired on roads, tracks and communication trenches round MARTINPUICH. Firing lasted throughout the night from 8·30 p.m. to 3 a.m.	
do.	29th		No 103 M. G. Coy. relieved this Coy. 1500 rounds were fired on enemy communication trenches. Coy. moved to camping area on AMIENS ROAD, ALBERT.	
ALBERT.	30th		Devoted to rest.	
do	31st		Devoted to cleaning of clothing, guns, limbers, equipment etc.	

1875 Wt. W593/826 1,000,000 4/15 J.B.C. & A. A.D.S.S./Forms/C. 2118.

Army Form C. 2118.

Vol 7

Instructions regarding War Diaries and Intelligence Summaries are contained in F. S. Regs., Part II. and the Staff Manual respectively. Title pages will be prepared in manuscript.

WAR DIARY

or

~~INTELLIGENCE~~ SUMMARY.

(*Erase heading not required.*)

Place	Date	Hour	Summary of Events and Information	Remarks and references to Appendices
			No. 44. Machine Gun Company.	
			WAR DIARY.	
			For the month of September 1916.	
			A. N. Colerke[?] Major, Cmdg. No. 44. M. G. Coy.	

2353 Wt. W2544/1454 700,000 5/15 D. D. & L. A.D.S.S./Forms/C. 2118.

Army Form C. 2118.

WAR DIARY

or

~~INTELLIGENCE SUMMARY.~~

(*Erase heading not required.*)

Instructions regarding War Diaries and Intelligence Summaries are contained in F. S. Regs., Part II. and the Staff Manual respectively. Title pages will be prepared in manuscript.

Place	Date	Hour	Summary of Events and Information	Remarks and references to Appendices
Albert.	1st 2nd 3rd		Training in machine gun work carried out	
Do.	4th		Coy. relieved No 45 M.G. Coy. in Divisional Reserve area at LONELY TRENCH, the DINGLE, near FRICOURT WOOD. Relief completed at 8.0 A.M.	
LONELY TRENCH.	5th		Coy. moved up to MAMETZ WOOD. 8 guns relieved guns of No 46 M.G. Coy., 2 guns being in reserve Line. Relief completed at 10.0 A.M. 3000, rounds were fired at enemy communication trenches and roads.	
MAMETZ WOOD.	6th		3,500 rounds were used in Indirect Fire on enemy communication trenches and MARTINPUICH.	
Do.	7th	4.30 am.	Remaining 8 gun teams of the Company relieved those in the line. 8.30 P.M. Several parties of enemy were seen leaving HIGH WOOD, and were fired upon by our gun in BETHEL SAP.	

Instructions regarding War Diaries and Intelligence Summaries are contained in F. S. Regs., Part II. and the Staff Manual respectively. Title pages will be prepared in manuscript.

WAR DIARY

~~or~~

~~INTELLIGENCE SUMMARY.~~

(Erase heading not required.)

Army Form C. 2118.

Place	Date	Hour	Summary of Events and Information	Remarks and references to Appendices
MAMETZ WOOD	7th	Continued	Parties were completely dispersed, and about 30 were seen to fall. 3000 rounds were fired by indirect fire on enemy tracks. Enemy retaliated, shelling trenches round gun position for about an hour.	
Do.,	8th		During operations of 1st Division and 44th Infantry Brigade against HIGH WOOD the two guns in BETHEL SAP were actively engaged, both during our Infantry attack and enemy counter attack. Good targets consisting of large parties of Germans at a range of 400 yards were effectively dealt with, and numerous casualties were inflicted. During the counter attack, one of these two guns was knocked out by shell fire. Indirect fire was carried on from 3.0 P.M. till 3.0 a.m. the ground to a depth of 300 yds., north of the tracks immediately east of MARTINPUICH being searched. Particularly heavy fire was maintained from 6.0. to 7.30 p.m. 14,500 rounds being expended. In addition to the gun in BETHEL SAP two other guns were knocked out by shell fire during the night. Aeroplanes observed very heavy casualties inflicted on enemy troops massing for counter attack as a result of this fire.	
Do.,	9th		The Vickers guns in BETHEL SAP were acting during operations against HIGH WOOD. Numerous casualties were inflicted on enemy as they retreated before our advancing Infantry. Indirect fire was used to enfilade tracks north of HIGH WOOD and to search ground N.W. of these tracks	

2353 Wt. W2514/1454 700,000 5/15 D. D. & L. A.D.S.S./Forms/C. 2118.

Instructions regarding War Diaries and Intelligence Summaries are contained in F. S. Regs., Part II. and the Staff Manual respectively. Title pages will be prepared in manuscript.

WAR DIARY

~~or~~

~~INTELLIGENCE SUMMARY.~~

(Erase heading not required.)

Army Form C. 2118.

Place	Date	Hour	Summary of Events and Information	Remarks and references to Appendices
MAMETZ WOOD.	10th		This Coy. was relieved by 5 guns of 149. Coy. and 3 guns of 150 Coy. in trenches N. of BAZENTIN-LE-GRAND and BAZENTIN-LE-PETIT. Coy. moved to SHELTER WOOD. 4 guns took over gun emplacements N. of CONTALMAISON. Indirect fire was used on N. part of MARTINPUICH during night.	
SHELTER WOOD.	11th		Coy moved from SHELTER WOOD to LONELY TRENCH near FRICOURT WOOD. 4 guns in the line were relieved by 45 M.G. Coy.	
LONELY TRENCH.	12th		Coy. remained at ~~lonely~~ LONELY TRENCH taking over Headquarters of 45 M.G. Coy.	
	13th		Coy. relieved at LONELY TRENCH by No 45 M.G. Coy and moved to bivouac area W. of ALBERT on AMIENS ROAD	
ALBERT.	14th		Coy. moved back up to LONELY TRENCH into Divisional Reserve, relieving 45 M.G. Coy. Relief completed at 11.0. P.M.	
LONELY TRENCH.	15th		During the attack on MARTINPUICH, by the 45th and 46th Brigades Coy lay in reserve at LONELY TRENCH.	
	16th		Devoted to rest.	
	17		Coy moved to PIONEER REDOUBT near VILLA WOOD. 8 guns relieved guns of 45 M.G. Coy. in trenches right of MARTINPUICH. Casualties 2. O.R. wounded.	

2353 Wt. W2544/1454 700,000 5/15 D. D. & L. A.D.S.S./Forms/C. 2118.

Army Form C. 2118.

Instructions regarding War Diaries and Intelligence Summaries are contained in F. S. Regs., Part II. and the Staff Manual respectively. Title pages will be prepared in manuscript.

WAR DIARY

~~or~~

~~INTELLIGENCE SUMMARY.~~

(Erase heading not required.)

Place	Date	Hour	Summary of Events and Information	Remarks and references to Appendices
PIONEER REDOUBT	18th		69 M.G. Coy. relieved this Coy. in trenches to right of MARTINPUICH. Coy moved back to pt. E.S. 6.7.7. E. of ALBERT.	
ALBERT	19th		Coy. moved with Brigade to LAVIEVILLE. Movement completed at 3 p.m.	
LAVIEVILLE.	20th		Coy. moved with Brigade to FRANVILLERS. at 9.30 a.m. movement completed by 12.15 P.M.	
FRANVILLERS	21st		Devoted to cleaning guns, spare parts &c, and personal clothing and equipment.	
	22nd–30th		Machine gun and Company training carried out, special emphasis being laid on the following: gun drill (Sectional & combined) mechanism, immediate action, range finding, rifle and squad drill, and special instructional parades for N.C.Os.	

2353 Wt. W2544/1454 700,000 5/15 D. D. & L. A.D.S.S./Forms/C. 2118.

Vol 8

CONFIDENTIAL

WAR DIARY

of

44. Coy. M. Gun Corps

from 1/10/16 to 31/10/16

Volume IX

Army Form C. 2118.

Instructions regarding War Diaries and Intelligence Summaries are contained in F. S. Regs., Part II. and the Staff Manual respectively. Title pages will be prepared in manuscript.

WAR DIARY

~~or~~

~~INTELLIGENCE SUMMARY.~~

(*Erase heading not required.*)

Place	Date	Hour	Summary of Events and Information	Remarks and references to Appendices
FRANVILLERS.	1–5		Period of rest, during which Coy training was carried out. Particular stress was laid on the following subjects:– gun drill; march discipline; advanced drill; tactical schemes.	Ref. AMIENS 17 1/100000
				Ch.
"	6		Movement to BECOURT carried out.	Ref. ALBERT combined sheet 1/40000 Ch.
BECOURT.	7		The day was devoted to cleaning.	
"	8		Relief carried out of 68 M. G. Coy, 23rd Division in Right Section, LEFT SECTOR, III Corps. 8 guns taken over in the line:– 2 front line, 4 support, 2 reserve. Coy H^d Q^rs moved to the QUARRY, BAZENTIN-le-Petit, at S.8.d.8.9.	Ref. 57c S.W. Ed. 3A 1/20000 Ch.
BAZENTIN	9		3000 rounds used in indirect fire on approaches to WARLENCOURT.	Ch.
	10		2000 " " " " " "	
			Casualties:– 1 Killed – 4 wounded (2 attached from 8/10th Gordons).	Ch.
"	11		3000 rounds fired on approaches to WARLENCOURT between 1.20–1.60 A.M. and 3.10–3.25 P.M. Good observation obtained. 500 rounds fired at enemy party at M.17.b.2.7 approx. Only 2 seen to escape.	

2353 Wt. W2544/1454 700,000 5/15 D. D. & L. A.D.S.S./Forms/C. 2118.

2.

WAR DIARY

~~or~~

~~INTELLIGENCE SUMMARY.~~

(*Erase heading not required.*)

Army Form C. 2118.

Instructions regarding War Diaries and Intelligence Summaries are contained in F. S. Regs., Part II. and the Staff Manual respectively. Title pages will be prepared in manuscript.

Place	Date	Hour	Summary of Events and Information	Remarks and references to Appendices
BAZENTIN	11		4000 rounds fired during the night on approaches to WARLENCOURT.	Casualties: OR: 2 killed 3 wounded Ch
"	12		During operations on the right indirect fire was brought to bear on trenches & tracks behind the BOTTE. All enemy C.T.'s ~~[illegible]~~ searched during the operations and for an hour afterwards. Usual indirect fire was carried out during the night.	Ch
"	13		4000 ~~[illegible]~~ rounds fired on C.T.'s and roads throughout the night.	Ch
"	14		44 M.G. Coy relieved by 66 M.G. Coy. 4 guns lent to 68 Coy. Lt. A.N. CARTER (2nd in Command) left for ENGLAND. Lt. K.V. BARRETT 3rd WELCH Regt reported for duty as 2nd in command. Casualties: OR 2 wounded.	Ch
"	15.		Nothing to report. Usual training proceeded with.	Ch
"	16		" " " " "	Ch
"	17		" " " " " – 1 OR. wounded	Ch
"	18.		In connection with operations on the right 2250 rounds were fired at trenches on the high ground behind the BOTTE.	Ch
"	19		66th M.G. Coy. relieved by 68 M.G. Coy. H.Q.s did not change.	Ch

2353 Wt. W2514/1454 700,000 5/15 D. D. & L. A.D.S.S./Forms/C. 2118.

3.

WAR DIARY
~~or~~
~~INTELLIGENCE SUMMARY.~~
(*Erase heading not required.*)

Instructions regarding War Diaries and Intelligence Summaries are contained in F. S. Regs., Part II. and the Staff Manual respectively. Title pages will be prepared in manuscript.

Army Form C. 2118.

Place	Date	Hour	Summary of Events and Information	Remarks and references to Appendices
BAZENTIN	19		Relief was slow owing to the rain and bad condition of the roads. 2000 rounds fired on roads and tracks around WARLENCOURT.	d
"	20		2000 rounds indirect fire carried out.	d
"	"		" " " "	
			In addition, 1000 rounds on new German trench in front of BUTTE.	
"	21		" " " " "	
			Heavy hostile shelling interfered with indirect fire.	d
"	22		" "	d
"	23.		Position of indirect fire emplacement altered. 6000 rounds fired on list of target attached.	d App: 1
"	24		"	d
"	25		"	d
"	26		" 2 O.R. wounded	d
"	27		"	d
"	28		" 1 O.R. wounded.	d
"	29		" 1 O.R. Killed (attached 9th Black Watch) 2 O.R. wounded.	d

2353 Wt. W2544/1454 700,000 5/15 D. D. & L. A.D.S.S./Forms/C. 2118.

4.

WAR DIARY

or

~~INTELLIGENCE SUMMARY~~.

(*Erase heading not required.*)

Army Form C. 2118.

Instructions regarding War Diaries and Intelligence Summaries are contained in F. S. Regs., Part II. and the Staff Manual respectively. Title pages will be prepared in manuscript.

Place	Date	Hour	Summary of Events and Information	Remarks and references to Appendices
BAZENTIN	30		8000 rounds on same targets.	cl
"	31		" "	cl
"	16		Following addition to the establishment of the a Machine Gun Coy were approved:—	
			8 Ptes. per Section	
			1 Driver, 2 Draught horses, 1 limbered G.S. Wagon } per Coy.	
			The personnel to be transferred from units of the Brigade. Authority:- G.H.Q. No. O.B./181.	cl

2353 Wt. W2544/1454 700,000 5/15 D. D. & L. A.D.S.S./Forms/C. 2118.

INDIRECT FIRE TARGETS.

DAY. (i) X road. pk. M5d5'1 and M.11.a.6.4 and sunken roads 500
(ii) House M11b7.5 250
(iii) Bank M11d8'5 250

NIGHT. (i) X Rds in (i) 1500
(ii) House M11.b.7'5 500
(iii) X Roads M11b2'0 "
(iv) Bank M11c8'9 "
(v) " M11d8'5 "
(vi) X Rds M11c 8'6 "
(vii) " M11a 1'8 1000.

Targets were fired at alternately.

Army Form C. 2118.

Instructions regarding War Diaries and Intelligence Summaries are contained in F. S. Regs., Part II. and the Staff Manual respectively. Title pages will be prepared in manuscript.

WAR DIARY

or

~~INTELLIGENCE SUMMARY.~~

(Erase heading not required.)

Vol 9

Place	Date	Hour	Summary of Events and Information	Remarks and references to Appendices
			CONFIDENTIAL WAR DIARY of No 44 Coy. M. Gun Corps from 1st November to 30th November 1916 (Volume X)	

2353 Wt. W2514/1454 700,000 5/15 D. D. & L. A.D.S.S./Forms/C. 2118.

Instructions regarding War Diaries and Intelligence Summaries are contained in F. S. Regs., Part II. and the Staff Manual respectively. Title pages will be prepared in manuscript.

WAR DIARY
or
INTELLIGENCE SUMMARY.
(Erase heading not required.)

Army Form C. 2118.

Place	Date	Hour	Summary of Events and Information	Remarks and references to Appendices
BAZENTIN	1.		Indirect fire was carried out both by day and night. 4000 rounds were fired.	CL
"	2.		Gun teams in the line relieved by No 144 Coy	CL
"	3.		Coy HdQrs moved to BECOURT.	CL
BECOURT	4.		Rest and cleaning	
"	5		Indents and cleaning	
"	6		Coy. moved to BRESLE.	
BRESLE	7 – 31		Training carried out in accordance with programmes attached as	Appendices 1-8
"	25		2/Lieut F. C. GIBB wounded (accidentally)	
"	27		General Inspection by G. O. C.	

2353 Wt. W2544/1454 700,000 5/15 D. D. & L. A.D.S.S./Forms/C. 2118.

1.

PROGRAMME OF WORK							
TIME.	Nov 7th	8th	9th	10th	11th	12th	13th
8.30.	Sectional inspection (billets, guns, etc)						
9.0 -10.30	(a) N.C.O.s individual instruction under C.S.M. (b) Nos 1 & 2 under Section officers (i) Mechanism (ii) General. (c) Remainder of Coy description Drill and arms drill.			ROUTE MARCH — Bresle Henencourt Laviéville Amiens Rd Bresle X Roads D.3.b. D.4.a. D.4.d. D.10.a D.16.c D.21a	as for Nov 7th	Church Parade.	Combined advanced gun drill (traversing vertical search combined sight
10.45-11.45	(a) N.C.O.s Gun drill under C.S.M. (b) Remainder of Coy. Elementary gun drill under Section officers				as for Nov 7th		Immediate action
11.45-12.30	Saluting drill	Immediate action			Saluting drill		Judging distance Range finding
2.0	Cleaning equipment and guns				Cleaning		Cleaning

K Barrett Lt
for Major.

PROGRAMME OF TRAINING NOV 1916

[illegible]o 44 Machine Gun Company	Monday 13	Tuesday 14	Wednesday 15	Thursday 16	Friday 17	Saturday 18	Sunday 19
8.30	Sectional inspection (Billets, guns etc)						Church Parade
9.0	Company parade DRILL ORDER						
9.0 - 11.45		'A' Sect Range	'B' Sect Range	Route March	'C' Sect Range	'D' Sect Range	
9.0 - 9.30	Company Inspection	Combined		D.21.a D.20.b	Company inspection	Combined	
9.30 - 10.30	Company Drill	Gun Drill		D.27.b D.29.b	Company Drill	Gun drill	
10.30	Break			D.17.b	Break		
10.45 - 11.45	Advanced Gun drill	Elementary Stripping	Elementary Stripping	D.21.a 7 miles	Advanced Gun drill	Advanced Stripping	
11.45 - 12.30	Mechanism	Arms drill	Light tripod drill	Arms drill	Mechanism	Light tripod drill	
10.45 - 12.30	'A' Sect Entrenching	'B' Sect Entrenching	'C' Sect Entrenching		D. Sect Entrenching		
2.0 - 3.0	Immediate Action						
2.0 - 3.0		'B' Sect Arms drill					

K B Barrett [illegible]

No 44 M.G. Coy.	MONDAY 20	TUESDAY 21	WEDNESDAY 22	THURSDAY 23	FRIDAY 24	SATURDAY 25	SUNDAY 26
8·30	Sectional inspection (Billets, Guns, equipment)						
9·0	Coy. insp.	Route	Coy. insp.	Route	Coy. insp.		
9·15	Coy. Drill	March	Coy. drill	March	Coy. drill	Tactical	
10·0 –	Combined	"	Combined	"	Combined	scheme	Churc
10·45	drill	6 Miles	Drill	6 Miles	Drill		Parad
10·45	Break		Break		Break		
11·0	A+B Sects	Break	D+A Sects	Break.	C+D Sects		
11·15	Range	C Sect	Range	B Sect	Range		
–	C Sect	Range	B Sect	Range	B Sect		
12·30	Digging	A Sect	Digging	D Sect	Digging		
	D Sect	Digging	C Sect	Digging	A Sect		
	under	B+D Sects	under	A+C Sects	under	Kit and	
2-0	Section	Tactical	Section	Tactical	Section	Gun	
–	Officers	handling	Officer	handling	Officer's	inspection	
3-0	arrangements	Rifle drill	arr.	Rifle drill	arrangements		
3·0-3·30 LECTURE	Care of feet	Gas	Theory of fire	Indirect fire	Overhead fire	Discipline	
3·30 – 4·0	Immediate action for men backward in training.						

J Barrett Lt.
44 M.G. Coy

Special classes Nov 20-25

(A) Elementary

Consisting of 18 O.R's under 1 Sergeant and 3 Corporals for instruction in
General description
Mechanism
Immediate action
Elementary gun Drill

(B) Range taking

Consisting of 4 N.C.O's and 4 Signallers under a corporal

Both classes under supervision of 2/Lt SWATERIDGE

J Barrett Lt
a/Adjt
44 M.G. Coy

No 44 M.G. Coy.	MON 27	WED 29
8.30	Sectional inspection (guns billets etc)	
9.0	Company Drill	
10.0–11.30	Combined Drill	
11.45–12.30	Immediate action blindfold	
12.30–1.0	Lecture: Gas	Lecture: Indirect fire
2.0	Stripping	
3.0–4.0	Mechanism	

PROGRAMME OF WORK	TUES 28	THURS 30
9.0 – 10.30	Range: "A" Sect	Range: "C" Sect
	Digging: "B" Sect	Digging: "D" Sect
10.45–12.15	Digging: A Sect	Digging: C Sect
	Range: B Sect	Range: D Sect
9.0–12.15	Tactical handling: C+D Sects	Tactical handling: A+B Sects
12.15–1.0	Lecture: Care of feet	Lecture: Fire direction
2–3	Immediate action	
3–4	Points before during and after firing	

J.J. Barrett Lt and adjt 44 M.G. Coy

No. 44 M.G. Company	FRI 1	SAT 2	Special Classes
8.30	Section inspection	Section Inspection	under 2/Lt Schloss (A) Signalling (B) Range taking (C) map reading.
9-0 - 12.30	Route March with Transport	Tactical Scheme No 1 Limbers and	
2-4.	Company Sports	Cooks Cart	

J K Barrett Lt
and A/OC
44 MG Coy

Instructions regarding War Diaries and Intelligence Summaries are contained in F. S. Regs., Part II. and the Staff Manual respectively. Title pages will be prepared in manuscript.

WAR DIARY

or

INTELLIGENCE SUMMARY.

(Erase heading not required.)

Army Form C. 2118.

Vol 10

Place	Date	Hour	Summary of Events and Information	Remarks and references to Appendices
			Confidential War Diary of 44th Machine Gun Company from December 1st 1916 to December 30th 1916 (Volume XI)	

A5834 Wt. W4973/M687 750,000 8/16 D. D. & L. Ltd. Forms/C.2118/13.

Instructions regarding War Diaries and Intelligence Summaries are contained in F. S. Regs., Part II. and the Staff Manual respectively. Title pages will be prepared in manuscript.

WAR DIARY VOL XI
or
~~INTELLIGENCE SUMMARY.~~
(*Erase heading not required.*)

Army Form C. 2118.

Place	Date	Hour	Summary of Events and Information	Remarks and references to Appendices
				ALBERT Combined Sheet 1/40,000 W 28
ALBERT	1/12/16		Removed to ALBERT. Operation order attached	L.S.W.
"	2/12/16		Training carried out. Programme attached	L.S.W.
"	3/12/16		Training as per programme	L.S.W.
"	4/12/16		Training as per programme. 2/Lt WALDEN admitted to Hospital	L.S.W.
"	5/12/16		Training as per programme	L.S.W.
"	6/12/16		Training as per programme	L.S.W.
"	7/12/16		Training as per programme	L.S.W.
"	8/12/16		Training as per programme	L.S.W.
"	9/12/16		Training as per programme	L.S.W.
"	10/12/16		Training as per programme	L.S.W.
"	11/12/16		Training as per programme	L.S.W.
"	12/12/16		Training as per programme	L.S.W.
"	13/12/16		Training as per programme	L.S.W.
"	14/12/16		Training as per programme	L.S.W.
"	15/12/16		Training as per programme	L.S.W.
SHELTER WOOD	16/12/16		Proceeded to SHELTER WOOD in Divisional Reserve. Billets in ALBERT taken over by 144 M.G. Coy.	L.S.W. ALBERT Combined Sheet 1/40,000 X 22 a

2353 Wt. W2544/1454 700,000 5/15 D. D. & L. A.D.S.S./Forms/C. 2118.

Instructions regarding War Diaries and Intelligence Summaries are contained in F. S. Regs., Part II. and the Staff Manual respectively. Title pages will be prepared in manuscript.

WAR DIARY VOL XI

or

~~INTELLIGENCE SUMMARY.~~

(Erase heading not required.)

Army Form C. 2118.

Place	Date	Hour	Summary of Events and Information	Remarks and references to Appendices
SHELTER WOOD	17/12/16		Cleaning in preparation for trenches	LSW
"	18/12/16		Cleaning	LSW
MARTINPUICH	19/12/16		Move to relieve 45 M. G. Coy in the line. A + B sections move to MARTINPUICH	LSW
"			C + D Sections move to VILLA WOOD. Lt SWATRIDGE + 2/Lt JENKINS go into trenches left of LE SARS. Coy Hqrs. at MILL MARTINPUICH.	ALBERT Combined Sheet 1/40,000 M32
"	20/12/16		Lt SWATRIDGE fired on enemy working party at dawn and produced casualties. Indirect fire - 2000 rounds on enemy communications	LSW
"	21/12/16		Team relief. 2/Lt SCHLOSS + 2/Lt WINN relieved Lt SWATRIDGE + 2/Lt JENKINS respectively. Indirect fire - 2000 rounds fired on WARLECOURT and points M5c 5½ ½, M11c 3½ 2½, M4c 4 2, M9d 9 8, M11c 6 6	LSW Ref. GUEUDECOURT 1/10,000
"	22/12/16		Usual indirect fire on same targets	LSW
"	23/12/16		Section relief. C + D sections relieved A + B sections respectively. 2/Lt JENKINS + Lt SWATRIDGE relieved 2/Lt SCHLOSS + 2/Lt WINN. Indirect fire as usual	LSW
"	24/12/16		Usual indirect fire on same targets - 3000 rounds fired.	LSW
"	25/12/16		Team relief 2/Lt WINN + 2/Lt CUMMING relieved 2/Lt JENKINS + Lt SWATRIDGE. Usual indirect fire.	LSW

2353 Wt. W2544/1454 700,000 5/15 D. D. & L. A.D.S.S./Forms/C. 2118.

Instructions regarding War Diaries and Intelligence Summaries are contained in F. S. Regs., Part II. and the Staff Manual respectively. Title pages will be prepared in manuscript.

WAR DIARY VOL XI
or
~~INTELLIGENCE SUMMARY.~~
(Erase heading not required.)

Army Form C. 2118.

Place	Date	Hour	Summary of Events and Information	Remarks and references to Appendices
	26/12/16		Usual indirect fire at same targets.	LSW
	27/12/16		Coy relieved by 45 M.G. Coy in the line. Relief complete at 7.30 pm.	LSW
			Removed to SHELTER WOOD.	LSW
SHELTER WOOD	28/12/16		General cleaning at SHELTER WOOD. 2/Lt GROUND reported and is posted to the Coy as from this date.	LSW
"	29/12/16		Cleaning belts, guns, equipment, in preparation for the line	LSW
"	30/12/16		Training in use of gas helmets; and ordinary M.G. training	LSW

END OF VOLUME XI.

2353 Wt. W2544/1454 700,000 5/15 D. D. & L. A.D.S.S./Forms/C. 2118.

44 M.G. Coy

Programme of Work

Week Ending Dec 16th 1916

Time	Monday	Tuesday	Wednesday	Thursday	Friday	Saturday
8.30 am	Sectional Inspection including billets					Tactical Scheme
9–10	Coy Drill	Range Practice	Coy Drill	Mechanism	Gas Drill	
10–11	1A blindfold 1.2 Revolver Practice		Gas Drill	1A No 1 T 2 Revolver Practice	Gun Drill	
11.15–12	Gun Drill		Gun Drill	Rifle & Squad Drill	Cleaning Belts	
12–1	Lecture Gas	Cleaning Guns	Lecture Indirect Fire	Lecture Fire Orders	Lecture Care of Feet	
2–4		Cleaning Roads	Guns Inspection	Route March	Scrubbing billets	

10.12.16.

[illegible] Major
Cmdg 44 M.G. Coy

44 M.G. Coy. Programme of work Week Ending 9th Dec

Saturday 2nd	Monday 4	Tuesday 5	Wednesday 6	Thursday 7	Friday 8	Saturday 9
8.30 Sectional Inspection	8.30 Sectional Inspection	8.30 Sectional Inspection	8 – 10 Baths. Kit Inspection	8.30 Sectional Inspection	8.30 Sectional Inspection	9 – 9.45 Cleaning Billets
9 – 11 Cleaning Billets	9 – 10 Squad Drill	9 – 10 Coy Drill	10 – 12 Range Practice	8.45 – 1.0 Route March & Gas Demonstration	9 – 12 Range Practice	10 – 12 Sectional Kit & Gun Inspections
11 – 12.30 I.A.	10 – 11 Gun Drill	10 – 11 I.A. blindfold Nos 1 & 2 Revolver Practice	12 – 1 Lecture Care of Feet	2 – 4 Nos 2 Revolver Practice	12 – 1 Lecture "Fire orders"	
2 – 3 Mechanism	11.15 – 12 I.A.	11.15 – 12 Gun Drill	2 – 4 Route March	Remainder Cleaning Roads	2 – 4 Route March	
3 – 4 Cleaning Guns etc Refilling Belts	12 – 12.45 Mechanism	12 – 1 Lecture Gas				
	2 – 3.30 Route March	2 – 4 Route March				

[signature] Major
Cmdg 44 M.G. Coy

<u>SECRET</u> Copy No 2

OPERATION ORDER No 1

Ref. ALBERT
<u>Combined Sheet 1/40,000.</u>

1. The 44th M. G. Coy will relieve the 149th M. Gun Coy in ALBERT on December 1.

2. Coy will move as follows:-
"A" "B" Sections under Lt JENKINS
"C" "D" Sections " " CUMMINGS
Transport " " SWAFRIDGE.
A distance of 100 yds will be maintained throughout.

3. An advance party under Lt MUNRO consisting of [illegible] C.Q.M.S, 2 gunners and 4 signallers will move forward. Times will be detailed later.

4. Limbers will be packed tomorrow morning.

5. The strictest march discipline will be maintained throughout.

29/11/1918

[illegible] Major
Comdg 44 M.G.C.

DISTRIBUTION.

Copy No. 1 All Officers
" " 2 War Diary.

Instructions regarding War Diaries and Intelligence Summaries are contained in F. S. Regs., Part II. and the Staff Manual respectively. Title pages will be prepared in manuscript.

WAR DIARY
or
~~INTELLIGENCE SUMMARY.~~

(Erase heading not required.)

Army Form C. 2118.

Vol XI

Place	Date	Hour	Summary of Events and Information	Remarks and references to Appendices
			CONFIDENTIAL WAR DIARY OF 44th MACHINE GUN COMPANY from January 1st 1917 to Jan 31st 1917 (Volume XII)	

A5834 Wt. W4973/M687 750,000 8/16 D. D. & L. Ltd. Forms/C.2118/13.

Instructions regarding War Diaries and Intelligence Summaries are contained in F. S. Regs., Part II. and the Staff Manual respectively. Title pages will be prepared in manuscript.

WAR DIARY
or
~~INTELLIGENCE SUMMARY.~~
(Erase heading not required.)

Army Form C. 2118.

Place	Date	Hour	Summary of Events and Information	Remarks and references to Appendices
PIONEER CAMP	1/1/17		Relieved 45th M.G. Coy in Right Sector of Divisional front, night of 31 Dec/1st Jan.	Ref. ALBERT 1/40000
			Lt SWATRIDGE, 2Lts JENKINS & WINN go into the line.	X17 C 8 6
			Rest of Company to PIONEER CAMP.	LSW
"	2/1/17		Sectional relief 2/Lt JENKINS & 2/Lt WINN relieved by 2/Lt GROUND & Lt ROGERS.	LSW
			Indirect fire – 10,000 rounds on WARLENCOURT & points M11 c 6 6. M10 c 5 6 M11 a 1 6 M7 a 1½ 7 M5 a 3 1	LSW
"	3/1/17		Indirect fire 10,000 rounds on usual points.	LSW
"	4/1/17		Sectional relief. 2/Lt WINN & 2/Lt JENKINS relieved Lt ROGERS & Lt SWATRIDGE. Usual indirect fire	LSW
"	5/1/17		20,000 rounds fired on usual points, and also M5 c 5 5½ M11 a 6 5 M4 d 1 5 as	LSW
			enemy relief suspected.	LSW
	6/1/17		Sectional relief Lt ROGERS relieved 2/Lt WINN. 20,000 rounds fired on same points as	LSW
			enemy relief was suspected – Approaches barraged throughout the night.	LSW
	7/1/17		Indirect fire 10,000 rounds on usual targets.	LSW
	8/1/17		44 M.G. Coy relieved by 46 M.G. Coy. Operation order attached No 4.	LSW X 22 c 5 3
SHELTER WOOD	9/1/17		Cleaning at SHELTER WOOD. Indents for kit made out by Section Officers.	LSW
"	10/1/17		Cleaning at SHELTER WOOD. Pro Helmets exchanged	LSW
	11/1/17		Cleaning in preparation for the line.	LSW
ACID DROP CAMP	12/1/17		44th M.G. Coy relieved 45th M.G. Coy in Left Sector Divisional front. Operation Order No 5 attached	LSW X 17 c 8 5
	13/1/17		Indirect fire 15,000 rounds on points M4 c 3½ 2½, LITTLE WOOD, WARLENCOURT, M4 b 7 0	LSW
"	14/1/17		Indirect fire on usual points	LSW
	15/1/17		2/Lt JENKINS & 2/Lt GROUND relieved 2/Lt WINN & Lt MUNRO. Usual indirect fire 8000 rounds	LSW
	16/1/17		Sectional relief Operation order No 6 attached. Usual indirect fire. 2/Lt SCHLOSS returned from course at CAMIERES	LSW
	17/1/17		Lt SWATRIDGE & 2/Lt SCHLOSS relieved 2/Lt JENKINS & 2/Lt GROUND. Usual indirect fire.	LSW
	18/1/17		Usual indirect fire	LSW
	19/1/17		Lt SWATRIDGE wounded by a shell in the left arm while working in the CUTTING LE SARS	LSW

A5834 Wt. W4973/M687 750,000 8/16 D. D. & L. Ltd. Forms/C.2118/13.

Instructions regarding War Diaries and Intelligence Summaries are contained in F. S. Regs., Part II. and the Staff Manual respectively. Title pages will be prepared in manuscript.

WAR DIARY
or
INTELLIGENCE SUMMARY.
(*Erase heading not required.*)

Army Form C. 2118.

Place	Date	Hour	Summary of Events and Information	Remarks and references to Appendices
SHELTER WOOD	20/1/17		44 M.G. Cy relieved by 46 M.G. Cy. Operation order attached	LSh X22 c53
"	21/1/17		Cleaning and indents at SHELTER WOOD	LSh
"	22/1/17		Cleaning. Gas Helmets inspected & exchanged. Route march.	LSh
	23/1/17		Cleaning. Route March	LSh X17 c85
PIONEER CAMP	24/1/17		44 M.G. Cy. relieved 45 M.G. Cy in Right Sector. Divisional front	LSh
"			Operation order attached.	LSh
"	25/1/17		Indirect fire. 3000 rounds fired on WARLENCOURT & points M11c66 M10c56 M11a16 M5a31	LSh
"	26/1/17		Sectional relief. Operation order attached. Usual indirect fire.	LSh
"	27/1/17		Indirect fire on enemy communications	LSh
"	28/1/17		Sectional relief. Operation order attached. 3000 rounds indirect fire	LSh
"	29/1/17		Raid on the BUTTE M17a36 by 8/10th Gordon Hldrs. Co-operation by machine guns as per Operation Order No 11 attached. Enemy machine gun located in action at M10d50 and silenced	LSh
"	30/1/17		Indirect fire 10,000 rounds. Barrage on approaches to the BUTTE throughout the night.	LSh
"	31/1/17		44 M.G. Cy relieved in Right Sector by 5th Australian M.G. Cy. Operation order attached.	LSh.

A5834 Wt. W4973/M687 750,000 8/16 D. D. & L. Ltd. Forms/C.2118/13.

SECRET. OPERATION ORDER No 4. Copy No 12
by Major C. King
Commanding No 47 M. Gun Coy. War Diary

8/1/917

1 RELIEF. The 47 M. G Coy will relieve the 150 M. G Coy on the night of 8/9. Relief will commence at Sgt Snooks cellar MARTINPUICH M.37.c.2.3 at 4.0 P.M. Half company at PIONEER CAMP will move to SHELTER WOOD at 2.0 P.M under Lieut Wilson. On relief all teams will move to SHELTER WOOD.

2 GUIDES. One guide from each of the following positions to be at Sgt Snooks cellar at 3.45 P.M.

PIMPLE, HILL, D.E.L.F Nests, CUTTING, LE SARS.

3 TRENCH STORES. The following will be handed over at each gun position in excess of S.A.A and the usual trench stores.

only 6 belt boxes (except in MARTINPUICH)

only 4 pairs Trench boots (except in nests & MARTINPUICH)

Receipts will be obtained and handed to O.Room by 9 A.M. 9th Jan.

4 TRANSPORT. A limber will report at Sgt Snooks cellar at 7.0 P.M. (Teams relieved before 7.0 P.M will leave 1 man at Sgt Snooks cellar to load their gun, tripod etc.)

Two limbers to report at VILLA WOOD at 1.30 P.M.

Two limbers to report at PIONEER CAMP at 1.30 P.M.

Transport will be detailed by Coy Q.M.S to move necessary stores from ALBERT.

5 BILLETING PARTY. Lieut Swatridge and five men will move to SHELTER WOOD to take over billets at 12.0 NOON. Lieut Swatridge will take over 60 belt boxes and 20 pairs trench boots. Detailed report on huts to be made.

6 On Relief being complete the following will be sent

7 ACKNOWLEDGE.

[signature]
MAJOR
Commanding No 47 M. G. Coy.

SECRET. OPERATION ORDERS Nº 5. copy Nº 8.

By Major C. King

Commanding Nº 44 M. G. Coy.

Friday. 11. Jan 1917.

WAR DIARY

I The 44th M. G. Coy will relieve the 45th M. G. Coy on the night 12/13 Jan.

II OFFICERS. Lieut A.K. Munro will take over the guns in LE SARS and Lieut L. Shvem in MARTINPUICH.

III RELIEF. The relief will commence at the MILL. MARTINPUICH at 4.45 P.M. 'C' Sect will be at the MILL by 4.45 P.M. They will relieve guns as follows:-

Nº 9 Team JOCKS ALLEY Nº 10 Team CHALK TRENCH.

" 11 " FLERS. FRONT LINE Nº 12 " FLERS SUPPORT.

'B' Sect will be at the MILL by 5.0 P.M. They will relieve guns as follows:-

Nº 5 Team G. Post Nº 6 Team } H. Post

" 8 " MARTINPUICH Nº 7 " }

The remainder of the Coy will proceed to ACID DROP. CAMP at 2.0 P.M., under Lt C.J. Sainbridge.

IV TRENCH. STORES. The following list of Stores will be taken to the gun position. Gun, Tripod, 1st aid case, condenser, 6 belt boxes. Trench boots will be taken over but NO belt boxes. List of Trench Stores to be at H.Q by 8.30 A.M. 13 Jan. All teams to provide themselves with a pick & shovel by 8.30 AM. 13 Jan.

V RATIONS: all ingoing teams will take with them 2 days ration, and water cans which will be filled at Pipe head at MARTINPUICH.

VI TRANSPORT: 2 four horse limbers will ~~report~~ at SHELTER WOOD at P.M.

2 two horse limbers will report at SHELTER WOOD at 1.30 P.M.

3 two horse limbers will report at SHELTER WOOD at 11.0 AM to convey Stores to ALBERT.

VII CARRIERS 'A' Sect will provide carriers to 'C' Sect. 2 men to each Gun.

VIII BILLETING. PARTY. Lt Jenkin & 3 men will proceed to ACID DROP. CAMP at 12. NOON to take over billets. Lt Jenkin will make a detailed report on the condition of huts.

IX ACKNOWLEDGE

J.F. Barrett Lt for Major.

Commanding Nº 44 M G Coy

SECRET. OPERATION ORDER No 6 — Copy 5

War Diary

by Major C. King

Commanding No 44 M. Gun Company.

WEDNESDAY. 16th January. 1917.

I RELIEF:-

"A" Sect will relieve "C" Section on the night 16/17th January

No 1 Team to Relieve No 9 Team.
" 2 " " " " 10 "
" 3 " " " " 11 "
" 4 " " " " 12 "

Relief will commence from the MILL MARTINPUICH at 4.30 P.M.

II GUIDES:-

One per gun to be at Hd Qrs at 4.15 P.M.

III TRENCH STORES:-

Trench boots (ALL) and Six (6) belt boxes will be handed over. Gun, Tripod, and 1st Aid Case will not be handed over.

Receipts in duplicate to be obtained. Original to be handed in to Hd Qrs at 9 AM 17th.

IV RATIONS:-

Ingoing teams to bring 48 hours rations. 48 hours rations for "B" Section to be brought up by 4.30 P.M.

Also 48 hours rations for Hd Qrs, & 11 attached men.

V TRANSPORT:-

One limber to be at ACID DROP CAMP at 2.30 P.M.

VI ACKNOWLEDGE:-

J Bayetti(?) Lt for Major

Commanding No 44 M. G. Coy

Distribution

Copy No 1 — O/C
" " 2 — Adjt.
" " 3 — Lt. Jenkins
" " 4 — C.S.M.
" " 5 — War Diary
" " 6 — File.

Secret

OPERATION ORDER No 7
by Major C. King
Commanding No 44 M. Gun Coy.

Copy 13
War Diary

Saturday 20th January 1917.

1 The 46th M.G. Coy will relieve the 44 M.G. Coy on the night 20/21st January.

2 RELIEF, will commence from the MILL - MARTINPUICH at 4-30PM and on relief all teams to report at HdQrs the MILL. Lieut Munro will march the party from ACID DROP at 3.0PM

3 GUIDES:- One per gun to be at the Mill at 4.15 PM.

4 TRENCH STORES:- Belt boxes will not be handed over. Trench tools will be handed over. Anti Gas appliances to be carefully handed over, as well as S.A.A (5 boxes per gun) range cards, braziers etc. Each team will bring out its petrol tin & pick & shovel. Receipts in duplicate to be obtained and original sent to O.Room at 9.0AM on the following day.

A carrying party of 2 per gun = 16 men, will be detailed by the Coy. S.M to parade at the Mill at 4.15 PM. The carrying party of 2 men per gun detailed by 46 M.G. Coy will also assist in carrying out.

5 TRANSPORT:- Limbers will report at HdQrs the Mill as follows
One at 4.45 PM for Hd Qrs
One at 5.45 " " "B" Section
One at 6.30 " " "A" "

Transport for the removal of stores from ACID DROP and ALBERT to SHELTER WOOD to be arranged by Transport Officer.

6 BILLETING PARTY, of 5 men under Lieut [illegible] to proceed to SHELTER WOOD to take over billets at 12 NOON. Lieut Jenkins will hand over billets at ACID DROP CAMP, and obtain necessary receipts.

7 ACKNOWLEDGE.

[signature] Lt
for Major
Commanding No 44 M.G. Coy

Distribution

Copy No. 1 — O/C 44 Coy
2 — O/C 46 —
3 — Adjt.
4 — Lt Rogers
5 — " Swatridge
6 — " Cummings
7 — " Jenkins
8 — " Weir
9 — " Munro
10 — C.S.M.
11 — C.Q.M.S.
12 — File
13 — War Diary

Copy No.

WAR DIARY.

OPERATION ORDER No. 8

by Major C. King

Commanding No. 44 Machine Gun Coy.

Wednesday. 24th Jan. 1917.

(i) The 44th M.G. Coy will relieve the 43rd M.G. Coy on the night 24/25 January.

(ii) OFFICERS:- Lt. E. Rogers will take charge of the PIMPLE Sector
Lieut D.J. Munro will take charge of the LE SARS Sector.
Lieut L.E. Schloss will take charge of the NESTS

(iii) RELIEF:- Teams will be in position as follows,

No 16 team at D NEST No 15 team at E Nest
" 14 " " L " " 5 " " F "
" 4 " Anti aircraft L Nest
" 8 " at MARTINPUICH No 1 at PIMPLE
" 2 " MILL Right Position No 3 team at MILL Left Position.
" 5 " LE SARS TR Right position No 6 " LE SARS TR. Left position.
" 7 " CUTTING LE SARS.

Nos 9, 10, 11, 12 teams at PIONEER CAMP.

SIGNALLERS at VILLA WOOD

Teams will be at the CUTTING M at the following times.

5. 6. 7 at 4.30 P.M. under Lieut Munro (leave Shelter Wood at 2.30 P.M.)
1. 2. 3 " 4.45 " " Rogers } leave SHELTER WOOD
8. 4. 13. 14. 15. 16 at 5.0 P.M. under Lt. Schloss. } at necessary interval

The remainder of the Company will move to PIONEER CAMP at 3.30 P.M. under Lt. G.D. Cummings.

iv. TRENCH STORES - The following will be taken in by each team.
Gun, Tripod, First Aid, Spare barrel, Cleaning Rod, 6 belt boxes, a Condenser, 48 hours rations, tin of water, 2 pairs of trench boots. A list of Trench stores (Gas appliances, S.A.A, Range cards, triggers etc) will be sent to H.Q. by the officer i/c of each sector, on the following morning

v. CARRYING PARTY. A party of 2 or 3 men for each gun team except No. 8 will be detailed by C.S.M.

vi. TRANSPORT:- 3 limbers at 1.30 P.M.
1 limber " 3.0 " for H.Q. to move to VILLA WOOD.

O.O. No 8 (cont)

VI (cont) 3 limbers at 10.0 AM to move stores to ALBERT
5 " " 2.30 PM " " stores to PIONEER CAMP

VII BILLETING PARTY. Lieut Jenkins and N.C.O and 2 men will proceed to PIONEER CAMP to take over billets at 2.0 PM.

Lieut Winn will hand over SHELTER WOOD to the 45th Company at 12 NOON and obtain necessary receipts.

VIII DRESS FIGHTING ORDER cap comforter, cardigan, Towel & soap, holdall, iron rations, waterproof sheets and overcoats. 5 Sandbags to be carried by each man except those teams going to the NESTS.

IX ACKNOWLEDGE

[signature] for Major
Commanding No 44 M.G. Coy.

SECRET. OPERATION ORDER. No 9.

by Major C. King

Commanding No 44. M. Gun Company.

Copy No 11

WAR DIARY

Friday 26th January 1917.

(i) OFFICERS:-

On the night 26/27th Jan. Lieut Winn will relieve Lieut Munro.
" Grand " " " Rogers.

(ii) RELIEF:-

No 9 team will relieve No 5 team. No 10 team will relieve No 6 team.
" 12 " " " " 7 " on the night 26/27th Jan.
Relief to commence at Cellar MARTINPUICH at 4.30 P.M.
On relief teams to return to PIONEER CAMP, reporting at VILLA WOOD en route.

(iii) GUIDES:- Lieut Munro will detail a guide to report to Sgt Richardson at the Cellar at 4.15 P.M.

(iv) TRENCH STORES:-

Guns and Tripods will NOT be handed over
8 Belt boxes per gun to be handed over. Receipts for all trench stores to be obtained and sent to H.Q next morning.

(v) RATIONS:- In going teams will take with them 48 hours rations.
All other teams and attached men will send ration party to cellar at 4.30 P.M. Officers to send servants.

(vi) TRANSPORT:-

One limber to report at PIONEER CAMP at 2.0 P.M to carry gun kit for 9.10 & 12 teams, and rations to MARTINPUICH.

(vii) ACKNOWLEGE:-

KBarrett Lt
for
Major
Commanding No 44 M. Gun Coy.

SECRET OPERATION ORDER No. 10. Copy. No. 11

By. Major G. King

Commanding No. 44 M. Gun Coy.

WAR DIARY

Sunday. 28th. Jan. 1917.

(I) OFFICERS: Lieut Jenkins will relieve Lt Irvine in the CUTTING LESARS on the night 28/29th Jan. Lt Jenkins will report at VILLA WOOD on his way up at 2.0 P.M.

(II) RELIEF:- The following relief will take place on the night 28/29 Jan.

No. 15 Team will relieve No. 10 Team

" 8 " " " " 12 "

" 14 " " " " 9 "

On relief 9, 10, & 12 teams will proceed to the position vacated by their relieving teams.

Relief to report to Lt Jenkins in the CUTTING at 5.0 P.M. Teams 8, 14, and 15 will leave 1 man to hand over to 9, 10 & 12. They will then rejoin their teams. The 3 men of 11 team will return to PIONEER CAMP.

GUIDES:- Lt Schlors will detail a guide to be at CUTTING at 5.0 P.M to guide 9 & 10 teams to their emplacements. No. 12 team will proceed direct to the cellar.

TRENCH STORES:- Everything will be handed over except guns & 1st Aid cases.

RATIONS: All teams to send ration parties to cellar MARTINPUICH at 3.0 P.M.

K Bayett [illegible]
Major
Commanding No. 44 M.G. Coy.

DISTRIBUTION.

Copy No 1 — O/C	Copy No 8 — Sgt Brooks.
" " 2 — Adjt	" " 9 — Lieut Schlors.
" " 3 — Lieut Jenkins	" " 10 — File
" " 4 — " Irvine	" " 11 — War Diary
" " 5 — " Cummings	
" " 6 — Coy. S. Major	
" " 7 — C.Q.M.S.	

War Diary

SECRET [illegible]

OPERATION ORDER No 11
by Major C. King
Commanding No. 44 M.G. Coy

Copy. 7
WAR. DIARY

29th Jan. 1917.

(i) The 44th Inf Bde will carry out a raid on the night 29/30th Jan on the BUTTE DE WARLENCOURT and QUARRY, in M.16.b.9½.6. The 44th M. Gun Coy will cooperate.

(ii) Two companies of the 8/10th Gordon Highlanders will deliver the assault on a front from M.17.a.6.0 – M.16.b.9.0 at ZERO. They will commence to return to our lines at ZERO + 25 mins.

(iii) From ZERO till ZERO + 45 mins M. Guns will barrage all approaches to the BUTTE. Targets will be engaged as follows.

GUN POSITIONS	TARGETS	GUN POSITIONS	TARGETS
CUTTING. M.16.c.4.3.	BAPAUME ROAD between M.11.d.1.9. and M.11.b.7.4	DURHAM TRENCH. M.22.c.8.7½.	Exit from LOOS CUT M.10.b.9.4.
MILL. M.22.b.9.6.	LITTLE WOOD M.9.d.7.8 to M.10.c.2.8.	L. NEST M.28.a.8½.7. Off dugout.	Ground around dugouts in M.11.d. a line from M.11.d.9½.4 – M.11.d.2.8.

Each of the above guns will fire 1 belt during each 10 min, in bursts of 50 rounds. Detail attached.

(iv) From ZERO + 45 min till dawn M. Guns will keep all approaches to the BUTTE under fire. Targets will be engaged as follows.

GUN.	TARGET
CUTTING	BAPAUME ROAD between M.11.c.3.4. and M.12.a.3.9.
MILL.	ROAD M.11.c.6.5 to M.11.a.6½.3
DURHAM TRENCH.	ROAD M.10.b.5.4 to M.11.a.5.3.
L. NEST	as at ZERO a line
OFF DUGOUT	M.11.d.9½.4 to M.11.d.2.8.

Each of the above guns will fire 1 belt during every ½ hour in bursts of 50 rounds. – DETAIL ATTACHED.

(v) All officers will make thorough arrangements for concealing the flash.

(vi) All guns will be tested by firing half an hour before ZERO.

(vii) AID POSTS. – HEXAM ROAD M.17.c.2.5 and LE SARS X ROADS M.16.c.2.4.

(viii) ZERO hour to be notified later.

(ix) ACKNOWLEDGE.

M. Barrett [illegible] for Major
Commanding No. 44 M.G. Coy.

Distribution

copy no 1 – O/C
2 – Adjt
3 – Lt Schloss
4 – " Cummings
5 – Jenkins
6 – File
7 – Mr Dean

SECRET. **OPERATION ORDER No. 12.** copy 10

WAR DIARY

by Major C. King.

Commanding No. [illegible] Machine Gun Coy.

Wednesday 31st Jan. 1917.

(i) The [illegible] Machine Gun Coy will be relieved by the 5th Australian Machine Gun Coy on the night 31st Jan/1 Feb.

(ii) RELIEF. The relief will commence at CELLAR MARTINPUICH at 5.30 PM. On relief gun teams will proceed direct to PIONEER CAMP. Attached Infantry will proceed with gun teams to PIONEER CAMP.

(iii) GUIDES. 1 from BUTTE, 1 from PIMPLE, 1 " MILL, 1 " Each rest } will be at CELLAR at 5.15 PM.

(iv) TRENCH STORES. The following will be handed over and receipts obtained.

Boxes S.A.A.	Flapper Fans	Picks
Shovels	Gas blankets	Gun waterproof Sheets
Vermorel Sprayers	Range cards	Maps.
Sand Bags	Anti aircraft Fork	1 Petrol Can

All the following will be brought out by teams

Gun, Tripod, 1st aid case and condenser, 6 Belt boxes.

All receipts obtained are to be handed to Orderly Room by 9.0 AM on the following morning.

(v) Nos 1s. No 1 in each team to stay in until dawn Feb 1st. They will report to Sgt Shaw at the CELLAR on the morning of February 1st. Sgt Shaw will march them to PIONEER CAMP. ~~12 hours rations for Sgt Shaw & the Nos 1 to be sent up on the evening of the 31st Jan 1917.~~

(vi) TRANSPORT. The limber will be at the CELLAR MARTINPUICH at 6.0 PM for guns from the cellar and the NESTS (total 6). The limber to be at the cellar MARTINPUICH at 6.30 PM for guns from PIMPLE, MILL, LE SARS (total 6). Transport Officer to make arrangements for transfer of stores from VILLA WOOD.

(vii) ACKNOWLEDGE.

[illegible signature]
Major
Commanding No. [illegible] M. G. Coy.

DISTRIBUTION

COPY. No 1 – O/C Copy No 2 – Adjt

" " 3 – Lt CUMMINGS. " " 4 – Lt. JENKINS.

" " 5 – " SCHLOSS " " 6 – Coy S M.

" " 7 – C.Q.M.S " " 8 – Sgt Shaw

" " 9 – FILE " " 10 – WAR. DIARY.

CONFIDENTIAL

Vol 12

WAR DIARY

OF

44th Machine Gun Company

From 1st February 1917 TO 28th February, 1917.

VOL XIII

Instructions regarding War Diaries and Intelligence Summaries are contained in F. S. Regs., Part II. and the Staff Manual respectively. Title pages will be prepared in manuscript.

WAR DIARY
or
~~INTELLIGENCE~~ SUMMARY.
(Erase heading not required.)

Army Form C. 2118.

Place	Date	Hour	Summary of Events and Information	Remarks and references to Appendices
BECOURT WOOD	1-2-17		Cleaning	[initials]
"	2-2-17		do & Indents	[initials]
"	3-2-17		do & Refitting	[initials]
VADENCOURT	4-2-17		Move to VADENCOURT. Operation order attached	APP I [initials]
"	5-2-17		Cleaning & improvement of billets	[initials]
"	6-2-17		Training Programme attached.	APP II [initials]
"	7-2-17		do do	[initials]
"	8-2-17		do do	[initials]
"	9-2-17		do do	[initials]
"	10-2-17		do do	[initials]
"	11-2-17		Church Parade. 2/Lt W. R. FELL & O.S. A. MARKSMAN reported & are taken on strength of Coy.	[initials]
"	12-2-17		Detachment of Coy detailed for contact aeroplane demonstration at BAIZIEUX Remainder training	[initials]
"	13-2-17		Training. Programme attached	APP II [initials]
BEAUVAL	14-2-17		Move to BEAUVAL Operation order attached	" III [initials]
GEZAINCOURT	15-2-17		" " GEZAINCOURT do	" IV [initials]
FORTEL	16-2-17		" " FORTEL do	" V [initials]
HERICOURT	17-2-17		" " HERICOURT do	" VI [initials]
OCOCHE	18-2-17		" " OCOCHE do Notification received that Coy is placed at disposal of XVIII Corps as from 20th inst	" VII [initials]
"	19-2-17		Improvement of billets. Cleaning.	[initials]
"	20-2-17		Cleaning	[initials]

A5834 Wt. W4973/M687 750,000 8/16 D. D. & L. Ltd. Forms/C.2118/13.

Instructions regarding War Diaries and Intelligence Summaries are contained in F. S. Regs., Part II. and the Staff Manual respectively. Title pages will be prepared in manuscript.

WAR DIARY
or
~~INTELLIGENCE SUMMARY.~~
(Erase heading not required.)

Army Form C. 2118.

Place	Date	Hour	Summary of Events and Information	Remarks and references to Appendices
LUCHEUX	21-2-17		Move to LUCHEUX Operation Order attached. At disposal of XVIII Corps	APP VIII [illegible]
"	22-2-17		Cleaning. Baths & underclothes.	[illegible]
HALLOY	23-2-17		Move to HALLOY. Operation order attached. Attached to 175 Inf Bge	APP IX [illegible]
"	24-2-17		Gas drill with box respirators & P.H. helmets	[illegible]
"	25-2-17		Voluntary church parades. Orders from 175 Bge to be in readiness to move shortly after 5 a.m. Necessary action taken	[illegible]
"	26-2-17		Cleaning. Detachment of Coy moved to "F" Sector XVIII Corps to be attached for instruction to 147 M. G. Coy as from 27th inst.	[illegible]
"	27-2-17		Gas Drill. Cleaning.	[illegible]
BAILLEUVAL	28-2-17		Move to BAILLEUVAL. Operation order attached.	APP X [illegible]

A5834 Wt. W4973/M687 750,000 8/16 D. D. & L. Ltd. Forms/C.2118/13.

SECRET. **OPERATION ORDER No. 13** Copy no. 10

by Major C. King

Commanding No. 44 M.G. Coy.

War Diary

APP I

I The 44th M.G. Coy will move to CONTAY on February 4th 1917.

II TRANSPORT:- 7.0AM Lorry to be loaded with blankets at X roads by railway at BECOURT. 1 N.C.O & loading party to accompany it to C.Q.M.S, where all stores will be loaded up.

8.0AM COOKS CART & A3. at Coy, as advance party to CONTAY via MILLENCOURT & HENENCOURT. Sgt Piper to accompany & find lines.

8.30AM Nos 2 & 3, to be at Coy to be loaded with packs etc & return to Transport lines.

11.45AM. Transport will join Coy at CHATEAU BECOURT. C.S.M to detail brakesmen.

III The Coy will maintain an ~~interval~~ distance of ~~[illegible]~~ 100 yds behind the 7th Camerons. H.

IV The Coy will march in ½ companies at 100 yds interval. Hd. Qrs & A Sect. 1st half Coy. B & C. Sections 2nd half Coy.

V "D" Section will form an advanced and a rear party. The advance party & 1 limber for company Cooks & Cooks cart will be under Lt Ground they will leave BECOURT at 9.0AM.

The rear party for final cleaning of camp will be under D Section Sgt. They will leave at 2.30PM & report to C.Q.M.S in ALBERT on the way.

VI Lt Jenkins, Sgt Caddick & 4 Signallers will form a billeting party, they will be at TOWN MAJORS office CONTAY at 10.0AM.

VII All blankets will be rolled in bundles by 6.50AM. They will be carried and loaded in the lorry at 7.0AM.

VIII A loading party of 1 N.C.O & 2 men will accompany the motor lorry to Q.M. Stores. They will accompany the lorry to CONTAY, where they will unload.

IX PARADES

6.30AM Reveille. 7.10 AM Breakfasts

7.0 am Loading blankets. 8.30 - Loading Packs.

8.45 - Sectional Inspection. 11.15 - Coy parade by ½ Companies. Fighting Order.

C King

Major

Commanding No. 44 M.G. Coy.

Distribution

copy No 1 — o/c
2 — adjt
3 — officers mess
4 — transport officer
5 — Lt Ground
Lt Jenkins
6 —
7 — C.S.M.
8 — C.Q.M.S.
9 — File
10 — War Diary

44th M. G. Coy.

APP II

PROGRAMME OF TRAINING FOR WEEK ENDED 10th FEB 1917

DATE	MORNING 8.30 - 9.15	9.15 - 10	10 - 10.45	11.15 - 12	12 - 12.45	AFTERNOON	REMARKS { Work of Specialists etc
6-2-17	Squad Drill	Rifle Exercises Revolvers for 1 & 2	Lecture Gas	Saluting Drill	Company Drill	Special Instruction for men insufficient in:- a. Squad Drill b. Rifle Exercises c. Gun Drill d. Mechanism	1. Special Programme for Signallers 2. Transport to receive training in Riding & Care of Animals by Transport Officer.
7-2-17	Squad Drill	Rifle Exercises	Gas Drill	Saluting Drill	Company Drill		
8-2-17	Squad Drill	Rifle Exercises	Lecture Trench Feet	Saluting Drill	Company Drill		
9-2-17	Gun Drill	Mechanism	A&B Sects Range C Belt Filling D Range Taking	A&B Range C Range Taking D Belt Filling	A&B Range C&D Rifle Exercises		
10-2-17	Gun Drill	Company Drill	C&D Range A Belt Filling B Range Taking	C&D Range A Range Taking B Belt Filling	C&D Range A&B Rifle Exercises		

SECRET. **OPERATION ORDER No. 14.** Copy No. 6

by Lieut R. V. Barrett. War Diary

APP. III.

Commanding No. 44 M. Gun Company.

14th February 1917

I. The 44th M.G. Coy will move to BEAUVAL on 14th Feby 1917.

II. The Company will commence passing the starting point, Cross Roads ½ mile N.W. of CONTAY at 9.14 AM

III. The following route will be followed HERISSART – LEVAL DE MAISON – VERT GALAND Farm.

IV. A Billeting party of Lt. A.R. Munro Sgt Caddick & 2 Signallers, & one Transport man will report to STAFF CAPTAIN at the CHURCH BEAUVAL at 9.30 AM.

V. Distances of 400 yds will be kept on the march between Battalion & M.G. Coy with T.M. Battery.

VI. The Lorry is to be shared by M.G. Coy & T.M Battery in one journey. A guide will meet Lorry at Bgde HQrs CONTAY at 8.0 AM & guide it to Q.M. Stores. A party of 1 N.C.O. & 2 men will accompany Lorry. Lt Munro is responsible that the Lorry is met & correctly unloaded at BEAUVAL.

VII. Brakesmen will be detailed by Transport Officer.

VIII. A groom will be detailed by Transport Officer to keep in touch with Battn in front.

IX. DRESS. – Fighting Order with overcoats rolled.

X. An advanced party under 2/Lt F. W. Ground will leave VADENCOURT at 8.0 AM sharp. Advance party to consist of :– Cooks Cart & C.Q. limber Sgt Reid, Pte Richardson, Pte Speirs, Pte Reid, Pte Jack & Pte Cooper G.

XI. Water bottles to be filled. Bread & cheese ration on the man.

XII. 20 Blankets will be laid flat on the top of each limber under the limber cover.

XIII. PARADES:–

6.0 AM Reveille

6.30 – Breakfast

Blankets to be put on limbers.

8.15 Billet inspection by Section Officers.

8.30 – Company Parade.

R Barrett

LIEUT.

COMMANDING No. 44 M.G. Coy.

Distribution :-

Copy No 1 — O/C

2 — Hd Qrs

3 — CSM

4 — CQMS

5 — File

6 } — War Diary
7 }

~~File~~ APP V

SECRET. OPERATION ORDER No. 16.

by [illegible] Barrett
Commanding No. 44 MG Coy.

[illegible] 1917

1. The Company will move to FORTEL via HEM - FROHEN-LE GRAND - VILLER L'HOPITAL
2. The Coy will pass the starting point (Road junction North of R in COURCELLES and MEZEROLLES - OUTREBOIS road at 9.19 AM.
3. A billeting party (personnel as OO 14) will meet Staff Capt at the Church at FORTEL 9.30 AM
4. Distances (as OO 14).
5. One Lorry shared by T.M. Bty for one journey. A guide to be at GEZAINCOURT at 8.0 AM.
6. Brakesmen (as OO 14)
7. Dress (as OO 14).
8. Advance party, personnel as OO 14 to start at 6.30 AM.

PARADES:

5.0 AM Reveille
by 5.45 Blankets to be on limbers
5.45 - Breakfasts
6.30 - Billet inspection.
6.40 - Company Parade.
7.0 - March Off.

A. Barrett

Lieut
Commanding No. 44 MG Coy.

Secret OPERATION ORDER No. 17.

APP VI

by Lt. K. V. Barrett
Commanding No. 44 M.G. Coy.
17th Feby. 1917

i. The Company will move to HERICOURT on the 17th Feby 1917 via LIGNY, NUNCQ & X roads SW. of CROISETTE.

ii. The Coy will pass the starting point X roads 250 yds S.W of NUNCQ at 9.45 AM.

iii. Billeting party (Personnel as OO 14) to be at

iv. Advance party personnel (as OO14) to leave at 7.30 AM

PARADES

6.0 AM Reveille
6.55 Blankets on limbers.
7.0. Breakfasts.
7.40. Billet inspection.
7.50. Coy Parade.
8.0 Move.

Barrett
Lieut
Commanding No 44 MG Coy.

SECRET OPERATION ORDER No 18 | APP VII

by Lieut K.V. Barrett.
Commanding No 4th M.G. Coy.
18th Feby 1917

I The 4th M.G. Coy will move to OCOCHE 18.2.17.

II ROUTE via CROISETTE — FRAMECOURT — HERLIN LE SEC

III The Coy will pass the starting point S.E of CROISETTE at 9.10 AM

IV Usual advance party will be clear of HERLIN LE SEC by 9.15AM

V Usual Billeting party to leave HERICOURT at 7.30AM.

VI DRESS

Fighting order with rolled coats.

VII PARADES

	6.0 AM	Reveille
	6.30	Breakfasts.
by	7.30	Blankets in limbers
	8.15	Billet Inspection
	8.35	Company Parade.
	8.50	Company move off.

K Barrett
Lieut
Comdg No 4th MG Coy.

SECRET OPERATION ORDER No. 18 | APP VII

by Lieut K.V. Barrett
Commanding No. [illegible] M.G. Coy
18th Feby 1917

I The [illegible] M.G. Coy will move to OCOCHE 18.2.17.

II ROUTE via CROISETTE – FRANCOURT – – HERLIN LE SEC

III The Coy will pass the starting point S.E. of CROISETTE at 9.10 AM

IV Usual advance party will be clear of HERLIN LE SEC by 9.15 AM

V Usual Billeting party to leave HERICOURT at 7.30 AM

VI DRESS
fighting order with rolled coats.

VII PARADES

	6.0 AM	Reveille
	6.30 –	Breakfasts
by	7.30 –	Blankets in limbers
	8.15 –	Billet Inspection
	8.35 –	Company Parade
	8.50 –	Company move off

[signature]

Comdg No. [illegible] M.G. Coy

APP IV

[illegible] ORDER No. [illegible]

by Lt. [illegible] Barrett

Commanding No. [illegible] Coy

16th Feb 1917

1. The Company will move to [illegible] on 18th [illegible] 1917.

2. Coy will pass starting point [illegible] 250 yds S.W. of [illegible] at [illegible]

3. [illegible]

4. [illegible] Party ([illegible]) will be at Town [illegible] [illegible] at [illegible]

5. Distances as O.O. [illegible]

6. The Lorry [illegible] by [illegible] Coy [illegible] for the journey. A guide to be [illegible] to meet lorry at 12 noon.

7. Breakfasts (as O.O. [illegible])

8. [illegible] (O.O. [illegible])

9. Advance party personnel as in O.O. [illegible] to start at 8.45 A.M.

10. Blankets as O.O. [illegible]

11. Parades

6.30 Reveille

7.0 Breakfasts

by 7.30 Blankets [illegible]

8.0 – 8.30 A.M. [illegible] feet [illegible] boots

8.30 – 9.0 [illegible] inspection

9.0 – 9.30 [illegible]

9.45 A.M. [illegible]

[illegible]

10.15 A.M. Coy Parade

H. Barrett

Comdg No. [illegible] Coy

SECRET. OPERATION ORDER. No 19 copy No 6

War Diary APP VIII

by Major C. King

Commanding No 44th M. Gun Coy.

Wednesday. 21st. Feby 1917

I The 44th M. Gun Company will move to LUCHEUX on 21. 2. 17.

II ROUTE: BUNEVILLE - MONCHEAUX - HOUVIN HOUVIGNEUL - ETRÉE - X roads 500 yds North of MAISON FORESTIERE - LE SOUICH - LUCHEUX.

III Billeting party Lt. A.N. Munro, Sgt Caddick & 3 Singallers to report to TOWN MAJOR, LUCHEUX at 11. 0 AM.

IV Motor lorry will be at Q. Mst Stores at 7. 0 AM. Blankets to be rolled & loaded on lorry by 7. 10 AM, also grooms horse blankets. 1 N.C.O & 2 men will be detailed by the Coy. SM to accompany lorry.

V Usual advance party will leave at 7. 0 AM.

VI DRESS: Fighting order with overcoats rolled & Steel helmets.

VII Water bottles filled. Bread & cheese ration on the man.

VIII Strictest march discipline will be maintained & any failure to comply with this will be severely dealt with.

IX PARADES.

5.30 ~~5.30~~ AM. Reveille

6.0 - Breakfasts

7.15 - Billet Inspection by Section Officers.

7.45 - Company Parade.

8.0 - Company Move off.

X All limber packing will be carried out in accordance with detail to be issued by the Transport Officer.

[signature]
Major
Commanding No. 44 M.G. Coy.

Distribution

Copy No. 1 — O/C
2 — Headquarters
3 — CSM
4 — CQMS
5 — File
6 }
7 } — War Diary

APP IX

SECRET OPERATION ORDER No. 20 Copy No. 2

by Major C King

Commanding No. 44 M.G. Coy

War Diary

Friday. 23. July 1917.

I 44th M. Gun Coy will proceed to HALLOY (distance about 4 miles) at 10.30 AM. Route – L'ESPERANCE. Reference map LENS sheet 11 – 1/100.000

II Usual advance party will leave at 9.30 AM.
Usual billeting party will leave at 10.0 AM, & report to Staff Captain 175th Brigade.

III PARADES:- as detailed.

10.15 AM. Company Inspection

10.30 – Move off

IV DRESS:- Fighting order with rolled overcoats.

V TRANSPORT:- T. Officer will make all arrangements.

VI Surplus Q.M's Stores will be left behind, under a guard of 1 N.C.O & 3 men.

VII G.S. Waggon will accompany transport to carry officers kits.

The C.Q.M.S will make arrangements to draw rations.

9th M.G. Coy will be at SOUASTRE.

C King
Major
Commanding No. 44 M.G. Coy.

Distribution

copy No 1 – O/C
2 – Head Qrs
3 – CSM
4 – CQMS.
5 – File
6 } War Diary
7 }

SECRET. OPERATION ORDER No 21 Copy. 6

War Diary

by Major C King

Commanding No 44 M. G. Coy.

APP X

Feby 28th 1917.

I ~~The Coy will move to LA CAUCHIE on 28th Feby 1917, via POMMERA – MONDICOURT – PAS – GAUDIEMPRE~~

II DRESS:- Fighting order with rolled great coats.

III Blankets to be laid flat on top of limbers.

IV A G.S. wagon will report at Hd Qrs at 7.30 AM to convey Q.M. Stores to BAILLEULVAL

V TRANSPORT:

All arrangements to be made by Transport officer.

VI Brakesmen to be detailed by T.O.

VII BILLETING Party of 4 signallers under L/C Ground to leave at 8.15 AM

VIII PARADES.

6.30 AM. Reveille

by 7.30 - Blankets to be on limbers.

7.45 - Breakfasts.

8.45 - Billet inspection.

9.15 - Company Parade

[signature]

LIEUT

for MAJOR.

COMMANDING No 44 M. G. Coy.

I For Para I Read:-

The Coy will move to BAILLEULVAL on 28th Feb 1917 via POMMERA + the T in station at BAILLEULVAL.

C

Distribution

copy No. 1 — Lt Barrett
2 — Headquarters
3 — C.S.M.
4 — CQMS
~~5 — File~~
6 }
7 } — War Diary

Vol 13

CONFIDENTIAL

WAR DIARY

OF

44 MACHINE GUN COMPANY

FROM 1st March 1917 TO 31st March 1917

Volume XIV

Instructions regarding War Diaries and Intelligence Summaries are contained in F. S. Regs., Part II. and the Staff Manual respectively. Title pages will be prepared in manuscript.

WAR DIARY

~~or~~

~~INTELLIGENCE SUMMARY.~~

(*Erase heading not required.*)

Army Form C. 2118.

Place	Date	Hour	Summary of Events and Information	Remarks and references to Appendices
FERMONT	1-3-17		Company relieved No 147 M. Gun Company in F Sector XVIII Corps. Company H.Q. established at FERMONT. Transport lines at BAILLEULVAL. Operation order attached.	APP I
"	2-3-17		Nothing to Report	
"	3-3-17		do	
"	4-3-17		1250 rounds fired at enemy aircraft	
"	5-3-17		1000 rounds indirect fire on Batt H.Q. and dumps at FICHEUX	
"	6-3-17		120 rounds fired at enemy aircraft. 1000 rounds indirect fire on Railhead and X Roads east of FICHEUX. Company took over (in addition to F Sector) Sectors D1 and D2 from 9th M. Gun Company. Operation order attached.	APP II
"	7-3-17		1000 indirect fire on X Rds and communication trenches in rear of German lines. One other rank No 60152 died of wounds accidentally inflicted.	
"	8-3-17		1000 rounds indirect fire on light railway and sunken road at BLAIREVILLE.	
"	9-3-17		50 rounds fired on enemy aircraft. 1000 rounds indirect fire on railhead and dumps in BLAIREVILLE quarry.	
"	10-3-17		1250 rounds indirect fire on X Roads and dumps at BLAIREVILLE	
"	11-3-17		500 rounds fired at enemy aircraft. 1000 rounds indirect fire on same targets as 10-3-17.	
"	12-3-17		1500 rounds indirect fire at intervals from dusk to dawn on gap cut in enemy wire.	
"	13-3-17		2500 rounds indirect fire on tracks and dumps at FICHEUX and BLAIREVILLE	
"	14-3-17		1000 rounds indirect fire on X Roads and communication trenches in rear of German lines	
"	15-3-17		150 rounds fired at enemy aircraft. 1000 rounds indirect fire at track and X Roads at TROIS MAISONS	
"	16-3-17		250 rounds fired at enemy aircraft. 1000 rounds indirect fire at light railway and X Roads at BLAIREVILLE	
"	17-3-17		1000 rounds indirect fire at track and X Roads at TROIS MAISONS	

A5834 Wt. W4973/M687 750,000 8/16 D. D. & L. Ltd. Forms/C.2118/13.

Instructions regarding War Diaries and Intelligence Summaries are contained in F. S. Regs., Part II. and the Staff Manual respectively. Title pages will be prepared in manuscript.

WAR DIARY
~~or~~
INTELLIGENCE SUMMARY.

(Erase heading not required.)

Army Form C. 2118.

Place	Date	Hour	Summary of Events and Information	Remarks and references to Appendices
FERMONT	18·3·17		Germans retired along Sector front. Outpost line of 8 guns established roughly on line of old German 3rd line and beyond.	[illegible] APP. 3.
BLAIREVILLE	19·3·17		Company moved to BLAIREVILLE by H.Q. established in quarry. Transport lines at FERMONT. Outpost line maintained. Operation order attached.	[illegible] APP. 4
FERMONT	20·3·17		Company returned to billets at FERMONT. Outpost line withdrawn.	[illegible]
"	21·3·17		Cleaning and refitting	[illegible]
DUISANS	22·3·17		Company moved to DUISANS and rejoined 44th Inf Bde	[illegible] APP. 5
"	23·3·17		Cleaning	[illegible]
"	24·3·17		Cleaning & refitting	[illegible]
"	25·3·17		Church Parades and belt filling	[illegible]
"	26·3·17		Fatigue Parties under orders of Town Major.	[illegible]
"	27·3·17		Fatigue Parties as on 26·3·17. Gun teams practised in open order movement.	[illegible]
"	28·3·17		Gun teams practised in moving in open order	[illegible]
"	29·3·17		Nothing to Report	[illegible]
ARRAS	30·3·17		Company moved to ARRAS. Operation order attached	[illegible] APP. 6.
"	31·3·17		Company took over 'A' 'F' & 'G' positions (4 guns). A & D Sections (Barrage guns) came under command of Capt. Morrogh M.C. Operation Order attached.	[illegible] APP. 6.

A5834 Wt. W4973/M687 750,000 8/16 D. D. & L. Ltd. Forms/C.2118/13.

War Diary

SECRET

OPERATION ORDER No 22

APP. 1

by Major King
Commanding No 44 M G Coy
Thursday 1st Mar 1917

I The 44th M G Coy will relieve the 147th M G Coy on the 1st Mar 1917.

II GUIDES

Guides to be at Coy Hd Qts by 10 AM.

III TRANSPORT:-

The transport of blankets & packs to be arranged by T.O.

IV PARADES:

6 30 AM Reveille
by 7 15 - Blankets in limbers
7. 30 - Breakfasts
8. 20 - Company Parade
8. 30 - March Off.

[signature]
Lieut
for Major
Commanding No 44 M G Coy.

APP 2

Copy 10

SECRET OPERATION ORDER Nº 23.
by Major Ching
Commanding Nº 44 M.G. Coy.

War Diary

Monday 5th 3.1917

1. The 44th M.G. Coy will take over the area of the 9th M.G. Coy tomorrow 6th 3.17.

2. Re-distribution to take place forthwith. "C" Section will vacate R 2 & R5 and occupy V 8 & V 6. "D" Section will vacate M.G 1 and M.G. 2, & occupy V 1 and alternate V 3.

GUIDES to be provided by Section in the VILLAGE LINE, to report on receipt of these orders. Relief to be completed as soon as possible. Section Sergts to come back temporarily to Village Line, to take over Section Stores. In addition "C" Section will detail one officer to take over Hd. Qrs at WAILLY.

"A" & "B" Sections will evacuate all their positions on completion of the above mentioned relief. A & B Sections complete to report to Coy H.Qrs tomorrow morning 6.3.17 at 7.15 AM. On completion of this relief, "C" Sect will have 2 guns in reserve line and one officer. One officer and 2 gunteams at WAILLY with definite orders to occupy V 8 & V 6. "A" Section will have 1 officer & 2 guns in reserve line 2 guns and Section Sergeant in WHIZ-BANG VILLA with definite orders to occupy V 1 and V 3 alternative if necessary. A & B Sections will proceed at 7.30 AM to take over positions held at present by 9th M.G. Coy.

RATIONS: "C" Section at WAILLY. "D" Sect & Coy Hd Qrs at Rivière. "A" & "B" Section will be rationed at a point to be notified later.

TRANSPORT T.O. to detail 2 limbers for each of "A" & "B" Sections, to report as follows 2 limbers B Sect WAILLY at 5.0 AM.
2 " A " SUGAR FACTORY at 6.30 AM

Packs & blankets of "B" Section will be put in the charge of the gun team in ~~CORNER HOUSE~~ ORCHARD POST. "A" Section will be stored in the charge of the gun team in CORNER HOUSE.

In taking over "B" Sect will take over the left of the 9th M.G. Coy. "A" Section will take over the right.

Completion of relief to be reported to Coy. Hd. Qrs by runner, when instructions will be issued about rationing.

Ching Major
Commanding Nº 44 M.G. Coy.

Distribution

Copy No 1 Headquarters
2 Section officer A
3 " " B
4 " " C
5 " " D
6 Transport officer
7 C S M
8 C.Q.M.S
9 File
10 } War Diary
11 }

SECRET Addendum No 1 to O.O. 23

Ref BEAUMETZ Map 1:10000 Edition 1A.

Rations for "A" & "B" Sections will be at old 9th MG Coy HQrs

GROSVILLE Point R25 d 7.2 approx (point from which relief commenced this morning) at 5.30 PM.

1 man per gun team to meet limber at this point

War Diary

[signature] Major

Comdg No [illegible] MG Coy

"A" Form.

Army Form C.2121
(in pads of 100).

MESSAGES AND SIGNALS.

No. of Message..........

Prefix .... Code .... m.	Words	Charge	This message is on a/c of:	Recd. at .... m.
Office of Origin and Service Instructions.	Sent		.... Service.	Date ....
	At........m.			From ....
	To			
	By		(Signature of "Franking Officer.")	By ....

TO

Sender's Number.	Day of Month.	In reply to Number.	AAA
*			

Distribution

as for O.O 23.

From

Place

Time

The above may be forwarded as now corrected. (Z)

Censor. Signature of Addressor or person authorised to telegraph in his name.

* This line should be erased if not required.

750,000. W 2183 –M509. H. W. & V., Ld. 6/16.

SECRET OPERATION ORDER No 25. Copy. 8
by Major Craig War Diary
Commanding No 44 M.G. Coy.
18/3/1917. APP 3

1 The following will be the distribution of Vickers guns.

No 1	- X 4 d. 1. 8	A Section under 2/Lt Jenkins. Officers H.Qrs QUARRY. in R34.d.
2	- X 4 d. 3. 8½	
3	- R34 d. 8. 3	
4	- R34 d. 8½. 3½	
5	- R35 a. 5. 2	C Section under 2/Lt Fell. Officers H.Qrs R35.a.5.2.
6	- R35 b. 1. 6	
7	- M 19. c. 6½. 4	"C" Section under 2/Lt Cumming. Officers H.Q. M.19.c.6½.4.
8	- M 19. c. 6. 6	

2 "B" & "D" Sections will be at a quarter of an hours notice to move in Fermont.

3 "B" Section will withdraw forthwith.

4 "D" Section gun in BOUNDARY POST to withdraw forthwith.

5 2/Lt W.R. Fell & "C" Section guns at present in R4 and R5 will relieve 2/Lt Cumming & the 2 "D" Section Guns near FICHEUX MILL at dawn 19/3/17.
Guides from "D" Section, 1 per gun will be at CRUCIFIX R23 c. 7. 7 at 5.0AM where they will meet teams of "C" Section.
A limber will be at R29. d. 1. 9 at 7.0AM to bring back "D" Sect's guns which will return to FERMONT on relief. "D" Section gun at R29. d 9. 9. will not be relieved, but will withdraw when the other 2 guns are relieved.

Distribution

Copy No. 2 – Headquarters
1 – O/C
3 – A Section
4 – B "
5 – C "
6 – D "
7 – } War
8 – } Diary
9 – File

O.O. No 25 (Cont)

6 Outpost line will be taken up on receipt of orders as follows.

2/9th Bn from Cross roads X.10.b.8.2 to road junction X 5 b. 5.4.

2/10th Bn from road junction X 5 b. 5.4 to enemy second line trench at M32. C. 6. 2.

2/12th Bn. Along enemy second line trench from M32. C. 6. 2. to junction with 89th Brigade at MADELINE. REDOUBT. (exclusive to 89th Bde).

7 Not more than one company of each battalion will be employed on outpost. The remainder of the Bttn should be given as much rest as possible, 2 companies of the 2/9th Bn being withdrawn to billets at RIVIERE on receipt of this order and one company of the 2/12th Bttn to Billets at WAILLY. One Company of the 2/10th Bttn to billets at LE.FERMONT.

8 The 173rd Inf Bgde will be on the right of the 2/9th Bn & will join them at X10. b. 8.2.
The 89th Brigade are on the left of the 2/12 Bn with their right about the MADELINE REDOUBT. Close touch must be kept with the outposts on right & left.

9 SALVAGE. Steps to be taken immediately by Sections in the line to carry forward as much material as possible from abandoned position.

J Barrett
for
Major
Cmdg No 44 M.G. Coy

Distribution

Copy No 1 – O/C
2 – H.Q.
3 – A Sect
4 – B –
5 – C –
6 – D –
7 – T.O.
8 – War Diary
9 – File

APP 4

Secret. OPERATION ORDER No 26.
by Major King
Comdg No 44 M.G. Coy.
19th Mar. 1917.

Ref Map. FICHEUX. 1/10000.

i Company will move to the QUARRY. BLAIREVILLE point R.34.d.

ii "B" Section will remain at FERMONT until 2.0PM when they will move to the Quarry.

iii All gun kit will be packed on No 1 limbers as soon as possible.

T.O will detail limbers to report to C.S.M. in order that they may collect gun boxes & other sectional stores not kept with the actual gun teams.

iv "A" & "B" Sections will be at a quarter of an hours notice for the next 24 hours ending 12 NOON tomorrow 20/3/17.

v Q.M. Stores will be in Fermont.

T.O. to arrange conveyance.

vi 80000 round (SAA) to be put in the QUARRY point R34 d today.

vii T.O will report at Coy H.Q. FERMONT on receipt of these orders.

C. King
Major
Comdg No 44 M.G. Coy

SECRET OPERATION ORDER No 27 Copy 4 | APP 5

War Diary

by Major C King

Comdg No 44 M.G. Coy.

Ref. Map.
LENS Sheet II. 1/100000

22 March 1917.

I The 44th Machine Gun Company will move to BERLES-AU-BOIS (distance about 5 miles) on the 22nd Mar 1917.

II ROUTE: BASSEUX - BAILLEULVAL

~~Ref. Map LENS Sheet II 1/100000~~

III A billeting party consisting of Lt Munro, Sgt Caddick and 2 Signallers will report to Town Major at BERLES-AU-BOIS at 9.30 AM.

IV Advance party under 2/Lt Ground will leave Coy HQrs at 9.0 AM. Party to consist of 1 gun team from each Section, cooks cart & C2 limber.

V. DRESS: Fighting Order with rolled greatcoats

VI Company move off at 10.0 AM.

C King Major

Comdg No 44 M.G. Coy.

Distribution

Copy No 1 - O/C
" " 2 - Adjt.
" " 3 - C.S.M.
" " 4 - War Diary
" " 5 - " "
" " 6 - File

SECRET ADDENDUM No. 1 to O.O. No. 27.

I Para I is cancelled & the following substituted "The 44th M.G. Coy will rejoin the 15th Division tomorrow 22/3/17, at LATTRE ST QUENTIN (distance about 8 miles).
ROUTE: BEAUMETZ — WANQUETIN.

II Para III. For BARLES-AU-BOIS substitute LATTRE.ST. QUENTIN.

III C.S.M to detail a guide to be at Bde Hd Qrs by 8.0 AM to guide motor lorry here.
This will be half filled by QMS. and then sent on to T.M. Btty.
C.S.M to detail one N.C.O & 2 men to accompany motor lorry as far as LATTRE St QUENTIN.

[signature]
Major
Comdg No 44 M.G. Coy

21st 3.1917

Distribution as for O.O. No. 27.

SECRET

ADDENDUM No: 2 to
O.O. No: 27

I In Para I Addendum No I for LATTRE ST QUENTIN
substitute DUISANS
ROUTE. BEAUMETZ – BERNEVILLE – WARLUS

II In Para II Addendum No I for LATTRE ST QUENTIN
substitute DUISANS

[signature]
Major
21st March 1917 Comdg 44 M. G. Coy.

Distribution as for O.O. 27.

SECRET OPERATION ORDER No. 28 Copy 4 1 APP 6

by Major C. King

Comdg No. 44 M. G. Coy.

30th Mar. 1917

Ref Sheets 51b & 51c 1:40000
51b NW3. 1:10000.

1 44th and 45th Infantry Brigades will relieve 46th Inf Bde in I.3. Sector on 31st inst, taking over right & left Sub-Sectors respectively. 7th Cameron Hgrs will take over Right Sub Sector before 12 NOON. on 31st inst. 13th Royal Scots will take over Left Sub-Sector after 12 NOON on 31st inst.

2 44th M.G. Coy will take over the undermentioned positions (4 guns) after 2.0 PM on 31st inst. 45th M.G. Coy taking over the remainder.

A G23d. 85.35., F G23d. 80.10. G (2 guns) G29b 83.75.,

3 'A' & 'D' Section will come under the orders of Captain MORROGH. M.C, from 6.0 AM 31st. Further detail will be issued for this.

4 Coy will move off as follows: 'A' Section 6.15 PM. Remaining Sections in order at 2 minute intervals. Distance of 200 yds to be maintained on the march. On approaching within 300 yds of the PORTE DE BAUDIMONT, box respirators will be worn in the "alert" position.

Fighting limber to accompany its own Section. T.O to distribute other limbers among Section evenly.

5 DRESS:- Fighting order with rolled overcoats. Picks & Shovels, petrol cans & at least 5 Sandbags per man will be carried on the Section limbers. Each Section will take these to its Section Billet on arrival in ARRAS.

6 T.O will arrange for the conveyance of valises, packs & blankets etc.

7 Q.Mr. Stores will remain in DUISANS.

8 Billeting party consisting of Lt. A. N. Munro, L/Cpl Henderson & 2 Signallers will report to the TOWN COMMANDANT, ARRAS at 10.0 A.M. A guide to be at the PORTE de BAUDIMONT to meet the Coy.

9 Relief of 46 M.G. Coy positions mentioned in Para 2 will commence at 2.0 PM 31st by 'B' Section. Detail for this will be issued on the morning of the 31st. 3.17.

C King

Major

Comdg No. 44 M.G. Coy

Distribution

Copy No 1 — O/C
2 — Adjt
3 — T.O
4 — O/C 46th M.G. Coy
5 — War Diary
6 — File

Account of Operations

2nd Phase

44th MGC.

April 1917

15th Div Artillery

Instructions regarding War Diaries and Intelligence Summaries are contained in F. S. Regs., Part II. and the Staff Manual respectively. Title pages will be prepared in manuscript.

WAR DIARY
~~or~~
~~INTELLIGENCE SUMMARY.~~

(*Erase heading not required.*)

Army Form C. 2118.

Place	Date	Hour	Summary of Events and Information	Remarks and references to Appendices
			Vol 14	
			CONFIDENTIAL	
			WAR DIARY	
			of	
			44th Machine Gun Company	
			from April 1st 1917 to April 30th 1917	
			(Volume XV)	

2353 Wt. W2544/1454 700,000 5/15 D. D. & L. A.D.S.S./Forms/C. 2118.

Instructions regarding War Diaries and Intelligence Summaries are contained in F. S. Regs., Part II. and the Staff Manual respectively. Title pages will be prepared in manuscript.

WAR DIARY

~~or~~

~~INTELLIGENCE SUMMARY.~~

(Erase heading not required.)

Army Form C. 2118.

Place	Date	Hour	Summary of Events and Information	Remarks and references to Appendices
ARRAS	1/4/17		1500 rounds fired at enemy aircraft. One plane brought down claimed.	
	2/4/17		Preliminary Instructions for Active Operations issued. 25% of the Coy returned to DUISANS under Lt. ROGERS & 2/Lt. F.W. GROUND (Ref LENS 1/100,000 I 3)	
	3/4/17		Preparations for active operations. Cellars in RUE DE DOUAI prepared for occupation.	
	4/4/17		Moved into cellars in RUE DE DOUAI. 1000 rounds fired at enemy aircraft.	
	5/4/17		Preparatory bombardment commenced. Very little retaliation. 4000 rounds fired from Barrage guns.	
	6/4/17		X day Bombardment still in progress. 4000 rounds fired by Barrage guns.	
	7/4/17		Y day Usual bombardment. Two casualties in A Section. Raid by 9th BLACK WATCH – A Section assisted with a barrage – 7000 rounds fired	
	8/4/17		Y+1 day. Final preparations for attack. Night firing from 8 pm till 1 am. to prevent noise of Tanks being heard by enemy.	
	9/4/17		Z day. Attack on enemy lines at 5.30 am. Preliminary Instructions & Operation order attached. Operations. Preliminary Instructions carried out. One gun under 2/Lt WINN knocked out – 4 casualties.	

2353 Wt. W2514/1454 700,000 5/15 D. D. & L. A.D.S.S./Forms/C. 2118.

Instructions regarding War Diaries and Intelligence Summaries are contained in F. S. Regs., Part II. and the Staff Manual respectively. Title pages will be prepared in manuscript.

WAR DIARY

~~or~~

~~INTELLIGENCE SUMMARY.~~

(*Erase heading not required.*)

Army Form C. 2118.

Place	Date	Hour	Summary of Events and Information	Remarks and references to Appendices
ARRAS	10/4/17		Coy Hqrs moved to RAILWAY TRIANGLE. Transport moved to ARRAS.	JSW
			Two guns under 2/Lt SCHLOSS moved to FEUCHY with 5/10th GORDONS.	
			Eight guns under 2/Lts JENKINS, CUMMING & MARKSMAN moved to HIMALAYA TRENCH.	
	11/4/17		15th Division attacked at 5 am with 44th Brigade in reserve.	JSW
			Two guns under 2/Lt JENKINS moved with 5/10 GORDONS & was relieved later by two guns under 2/Lt WINN. 2/Lt JENKINS then moved to a position west of MONCHY. 2/Lt WINN with two guns attacked with 5/10 GORDONS but were held up.	
			Lt MUNRO & 2/Lt FELL with 4 guns moved to Coy. Hqrs. 2/Lts CUMMING & MARKSMAN stayed in HIMALAYA TRENCH.	
			MAJOR C KING killed while visiting guns near MONCHY:— 5 O.R. casualties.	
	12/4/17		Coy relieved at 3 am by 51st M.G. Coy. The Company moved to FEUCHY and later to cellars in RUE DE DOUAI — ARRAS.	JSW
			MAJOR KING buried in cemetery RUE DE DOUAI.	
	13/4/17		Resting, cleaning, and refitting	JSW
	14/4/17		Resting cleaning and refitting	JSW

2353 Wt. W2514/1454 700,000 5/15 D. D. & L. A.D.S.S./Forms/C. 2118.

Army Form C. 2118.

WAR DIARY
or
INTELLIGENCE SUMMARY.
(Erase heading not required.)

Instructions regarding War Diaries and Intelligence Summaries are contained in F. S. Regs., Part II. and the Staff Manual respectively. Title pages will be prepared in manuscript.

Place	Date	Hour	Summary of Events and Information	Remarks and references to Appendices
ARRAS	15/4/17		Resting, cleaning & refitting	F.S.W.
	16/4/17		Visual Training & Recognition of Targets.	F.S.W.
	17/4/17		Nothing to report.	F.S.W.
	18/4/17		Cleaning guns; I.A. & Lecture on Overhead fire	F.S.W.
	19/4/17		Six guns of under Lt. MUNRO & 2/Lt. SCHLOSS relieved six guns of 57 M.G. Coy. near WANCOURT. Remainder of Company at ARRAS (Sheet 51BSW. N.23)	F.S.W.
			Advanced Coy. Hqrs at N16a97 Sh. 51BSW. 1	
	20/4/17		Indirect fire carried out	F.S.W.
	21/4/17		Indirect fire carried out.	F.S.W.
	22/4/17		Remainder of Company less 28/0 moved up previous to attack.	F.S.W.
			2/Lt. JENKINS with two guns attached to SEAFORTH HLDRS	F.S.W.
			2/Lt. CUMMING with two guns attached to CAMERON HLDRS.	F.S.W.
			2/Lt. MARKSMAN with two guns attached to BLACK WATCH.	
			2/Lt. GROUND with two guns attached to GORDONS	
			A & C Sections in Brigade Reserve	

2353 Wt. W2544/1454 700,000 5/15 D. D. & L. A.D.S.S./Forms/C. 2118.

Army Form C. 2118.

Instructions regarding War Diaries and Intelligence Summaries are contained in F. S. Regs., Part II. and the Staff Manual respectively. Title pages will be prepared in manuscript.

WAR DIARY
or
~~INTELLIGENCE~~ SUMMARY.
(*Erase heading not required.*)

Place	Date	Hour	Summary of Events and Information	Remarks and references to Appendices
	23/4/17		Attack on enemy lines at 4.45 am Operation order attached.	Ref. 51B S.W. N 18.
			2/Lt MARKSMAN wounded. Enemy M.G fire held up the advance	LSW
			GUEMAPPE captured, but lost again. Heavy casualties to Brigade.	
			Guns advanced with Battalions to which they were attached.	
			GUEMAPPE again captured & held. 44th & 45th Brigades relieved by	
			46th Brigade which advanced another 200x.	
	24/4/17		C Section and 2 teams of B section advanced and took up Barrage	LSW
			positions 200x W. of GUEMAPPE to support further attack by 46 Brigade.	
	25/4/17		Lt. MUNRO with two guns attached to BLACK WATCH – 2/Lt CUMMING	Sheet 51B S.W.
			with two guns attached to CAMERONS for a night raid on CAVALRY FARM	O.4.a 5.8.
			CAMERONS driven back by M.G fire. BLACK WATCH established posts to	LSW.
			South of farm. Lt MUNRO advanced & placed his guns 300x S. of farm.	
			2/Lt JENKINS with four guns took up position N19a Sheet 51BSW, & did	
			direct fire on enemy positions. Continuous fire from Barrage guns.	
			2/Lt GROUND killed while advancing with GORDON HLDRS.	

2353 Wt. W2514/1454 700,000 5/15 D. D. & L. A.D.S.S./Forms/C. 2118.

Instructions regarding War Diaries and Intelligence Summaries are contained in F. S. Regs., Part II. and the Staff Manual respectively. Title pages will be prepared in manuscript.

WAR DIARY
or
~~INTELLIGENCE SUMMARY.~~

(Erase heading not required.)

Army Form C. 2118.

Place	Date	Hour	Summary of Events and Information	Remarks and references to Appendices
	26/4/17		Situation unchanged. Barrage guns placed a barrage on S.O.S. line at 3.45 a.m.	LSW
	27/4/17		Situation unchanged.	LSW
	28/4/17		Barrage put on enemy lines at 4.25 am. as a blind – no attack.	LSW
			Relieved by 167 M.G. Coy – Operation Order attached. Withdrew to ARRAS.	B/LENS 1/100000 H3
	29/4/17		Removed with Brigade to SIMENCOURT. Operation order attached	LSW
	30/4/17		Cleaning & indents. L/Corpl G. GALLOW, SHANNON awarded the Military Medal.	LSW

2353 Wt. W2544/1454 700,000 5/15 D. D. & L. A.D.S.S./Forms/C. 2118.

TX. 3.

To
AR

Ref BM. 28

1. On the night of the 22nd I took the four guns I held in reserve at ARRAS up to Hdqrs at N·11·a·5·2. The night was quiet.

2. On the afternoon of the 23rd about 4pm I was ordered to get the guns up to assist the BLACK WATCH to take the CEMETERY. I took the guns over to Hdqrs at N·17·D·1·2. The journey from N·11·a to N·17·D was uneventful though there were occasional bursts of M.G. fire directed towards us.
Difficulty was experienced in getting amm as there was none at A.R.B.
After some time I got forty rounds with carriers so I went over with two guns each with twenty rounds.
On getting up behind the CEMETERY I found that we had already taken it and were digging in.
I found two of my guns and

hands with the BLACK WATCH so I arranged the four in defensive positions behind the line we had started to consolidate.

By this time the 46th D.B. were coming through us.

3. On the night of the 24th I sent up five guns to get into position to support the attack on CAVALRY FARM.

They were dug in in shell holes at approximately.

N.14.a.1.4.
N.14.a.1.2
N.14.a.2.4
N.14.c.1.9
N.14.c.½.7½

4. On the night of the 25th April we opened fire from the five guns at zero.

Two guns covered the advance of the B.W. on the right. They fired till zero + 3.

Two guns were trained on trench running from O.14.a.7.0 to O.14.a.9.3 these guns fired till zero + 6.

One gun searched the enclosures around CAVALRY FARM. This gun fired from zero to zero + 3.

In all over 200 rounds were fired.

Remarks:–

5(a) Throughout the operations it is worthy of note that not a single gun has been knocked out by the Enemy.

(b) The supply of amm. was a difficult matter as had been anticipated.

(c) A good few misfires occurred due to damp cartridges or defective caps

(d) In only a few cases did the guns with Battns. get into action.

(e) If at all possible it would be a good thing if Coy. Commanders etc sent information to the guns occasionally, telling them of any M.G. etc that were causing trouble.

G K W Stewart Capt
O.C. KV

1/5/17

Gwl

Statement of part taken by 44 Machine Gun Company in the operations from 19th – 29th April

—"—

19th Six guns relieved 87th M.G. Coy. on the ridge N.11.c.
Remainder of the Company in Rue de DOUAI. ARRAS.

20th Indirect and direct fire carried out on enemy's positions.

21st " " "

22nd Remainder of the Company moved into their positions prior to attack.
6 guns remained in position on N.11.c.
2 guns with 9th Black Watch in right half of "B" trench.
2 guns with 8th Seaforths in old front line N.17.c.
2 guns with 8/10th Gordons in Brown line N.16.a.
2 guns with 7th Camerons in left half "B" trench.
2 guns in reserve in Brown line N.16.a.

23rd. At Zero hour guns attached to battalions advanced with them.
2 guns with the Black Watch advanced to about N. 18. ~~b~~ 5. 2. but had to retire to our old front line.
2 guns with the Seaforths advanced to about O. 13. a. 3. 0 but had to retire to bank N. 18. c. 2. 5.
2 guns with the 7 Cameron Hdrs advanced to about N. 18. b. 2. 6. where they remained.
2 guns with the 8/10 Gordons advanced to ~~trench~~ just in behind the bogey line.
6 guns on the ridge in N. 11. c. opened fire on Sunken Road, O. 13. c. – X roads O. 19. a. ~~9~~ 9. –
At Zero + 1 hour four guns from ridge in N. 11. c. advanced intending to take up more forward position to cover further advance. These were caught with M.G. fire about the Old British front line.
One gun dug in good position in our old front line remainder withdrawn to old positions on ridge N. 11. c.. From where fire was carried out on observed and reported targets. Good effect was observed in O. 19. a.

24th. Guns on ridge in N. 11. c. advanced to positions on grid between N. 18. c. and d

to give indirect fire support to 46th Brigade
Guns withdrawn to Brown line N.16.a.

~~[illegible]~~

25th. 2 guns attached to Black Watch and 2 guns to Camerons for raid on Cavalry Farm. 2 guns with Black Watch pushed forward before the attack to a position O.14.c.4.5. 2 guns with Camerons took up position in O.13.b.3.7. from where they could give covering to the Camerons.
4 guns crossed R. ~~Cojeu~~ COJEUL and took up position in O.19.a. from where direct fire could be obtained on CAVALRY FARM and BOIS DU VERT.
The 6 indirect fire barrage guns fire continuously.
2 guns with the 8/10 Gordons advanced to very near the farm, these guns withdrew with the Gordons.

26. No movement of guns. Barrage guns fired intense at 3.45 am. on LANYARD TRENCH. And continued firing short bursts throughout the day.

27. No change.

28. Intense barrage from barrage guns on LANYARD TRENCH at 4.25 in

accordance with programme.

9 ~~Return~~ 4 guns in O.19.a. obtained some targets and claim several hits.

Relieved by 187 M.G. Coy and withdrew ARRAS.

2/5/17

J K Barrett Lieut

Cand 44 M.G. Coy

Points noticed During the Operations

The guns attatched to Battalions and pushed forward too early before the capture of any position proved of no value. As their fire was entirely masked by enemy machine guns ~~under~~ behind cover.

The guns behind on the ridge doing long range fire proved useful, and probably did a good deal of damage.

The best position for both supporting and covering an attack or guarding against a counter attack was the high ground on the flank as in O. 19. a.

Guns in positions as in O. 19. a should be in telephone communication with Coy. H. 2.

More use should be made of field glasses.

It is suggested that the guns attatched to battalions be in a position to give overhead covering fire, and should only advance to a position ~~that~~

then it has been captured.

1/5/17

K Barrett Lieut
Cmd 44 M.G. Company

Endg

SECRET PRELIMINARY INSTRUCTIONS for

OFFENSIVE OPERATIONS.

1 The 44th Inf Bde will attack the German lines between the following boundaries on "Z" day.
(a) on South. The road (inclusive) which runs through G.29a.45.85 — the CEMETRY - SUPPORT line - Front line at G30.a.65.80 - German line at G 30 b.15.75 - due E to H 25.a.5.8 - H.26.a.3.6 - H.28.d.1.1
(b) on North. Cross roads, G 23.d.70.15 - Railway crossing G23.c.85.35 - N of IVORY STREET - front line at G24.c.55.60 — 75 yds N of railway - H.19.c.1.85 — H 19.b.8.3.

2 The 1st Objective. H.25.a.3.8 through FREDS WOOD.
The 2nd Objective. H 26 a.3.6 — H.20.a 5.0. — H.13.d.8.3.

3 The advance to the 1st objective will be covered by an artillery barrage assisted by a M.G Barrage under Divisional M.G. Officer.

4 Preliminary distribution during V.W.X & Y days — Company H.Q, "C" Sect, Spare men A & D, in cellars 39-49 RUE DE DOUAI. — "B" Section in dugouts in the trenches. — 44th Inf Bde H.Q CEMETRY ROAD No 5. G 29.a.7.8.

5 Distribution at ZERO Hour — Company H.Q — ~~[illegible]~~ — 2 guns "C" Sect with Support Battn. in Cave No 9. 2 guns "C" Sect in I.R. line — A & D Sects under DIV M.G.O — Brigade H.Q no change. — B Section in their present dugouts.

6 Reserve of Personnel. Two officers Lieut Rogers & 2/Lt Ground & 45 O.R.s will be accommodated at DUISANS.

7 Brigade Dumps will be as follows.

A.R.A G 29.a.7.8 (cellars 1, 2 & 7)
A.R.B 1 G 29.b.8½.8½
A.R.B 2 G 28.d.8½.3½.
A.R.C G 30.a.5.9½.
A.R.D G.24.d.7.5
A.R.E. H.19.d.6.7

Stores will only be issued on written demand on WHITE cards issued.
2 Limbered G.S waggons & 8 Pack animals will be at the disposal of the Bde T.O. They will be picketed at G.13.b

8 DRESS. Fighting order. 2 days rations besides the unconsumed portion of the days ration per man. 100 rounds of S.A.A per man. 5 Sand bags per man. 1 Pick & Shovel per team.

9 Medical Posts at
G.23.d.2.4 advanced
G.30.b.6.4 - walking
G.21.b.8.8. lying.

10 WATER
5, 50 gallon tanks are disposed as follows.
No 1 in Rt front Battn H.Q. Dugout. G 23.d.5½.3.
No 2 " Lt " " " G 23.d.4.3.
No 3 - in dugout No 9 Cave.

SECRET (cont)

10 WATER (cont)

No. 4 } In Support Battn H.Q. cellar for use of troops in
No. 5 } RUE DE DOUAI.

Water is also being stored in each cellar.

11 COMMUNICATIONS:- The following are the position of Brigade forward Signal Stations:-

(a) Sap 64.
(b) P.B.1 along sunken road through G.24.d.6.4.
(c) along track S of railway to vicinity of Pt 78.

12 DETAILS:- 'A' & 'D' Sects under 2/Lieuts Jenkins, Cumming, & Marksman are at the disposal of Capt. MORROGH for the M.G. barrage.

'B' Section under Lieut Mauro and 2/Lt Fell will advance from their present dugouts & consolidate the 1st objective after the 2nd has been taken.

'C' Section 2 guns under Lt. Winn will advance behind the support Battn & will consolidate the 1st objective, passing through the Support Battn. They will then assist the advance to the 2nd objective by their fire. As soon as the 2nd objective has been captured they will advance & consolidate in the line of the 2nd objective; their place in the 1st objective being taken by 'B' Section.

'C' Section 2 guns will remain in reserve in Cave No. 9.

3 April 1917

R Barrett
Major
Comdg No. 44 M.G. Coy

DISTRIBUTION
Copy No. 1 - O/C
" " 2 - all officers.
" " 3 - War Diary
" " 4 - File.

SECRET ADDENDUM No 1 copy 3

War Diary

Preliminary Instruction for Offensive Operations.

13 CONSOLIDATION. The main line to be consolidated by the 44th Infantry Brigade runs along the northern of observatory RIDGE. The following are the strong points to be constructed in this line.

H.26.a.6.7 } 8/10th Gordon Hdrs
H.20.c.5½.½ }
H.20.c.5½.3½ } 7th Cameron Hdrs
H.20.c.5½.6 }
H.20.a.6.8½ } 9th Black Watch.
H 20.a.5½.1½ }

The second line to be consolidated by the 8th Seaforth Hdrs is the 1st objective (approx the line of GLENELG LANE from H25.a½.7½. to the Railway Embankment) "B" Section, 44th M.G. Coy are responsible for the selection & construction of their own positions in this line.

There will be a strong point at H.25.a½.7½.

14 TANKS:- Two male tanks will cooperate with 44th Inf Bde. They will advance 160 yds S of the Railway. One will cross the Railway at H.20.A.10.0 and deal with the Railway Triangle; FEUCHY LANE and strong points at N end of HELLE TRENCH. The other will assist the infantry and deal with W end of FEUCHY SWITCH and HART WORK.

15 RUNNERS:- all messages to Coy H.Q will be duplicated. When a runner arrives from the line he will be replaced by another runner; but will return with the next message.

16 BLANKETS and OVERCOATS:- will be sent to Coy H.Q. by 5.0PM on "Y" Day. To be stored in Brigade Store.

CORRECTION

Para (12) "B" Section under - - - - - - - - - - - - - has been taken;"

should read.

"B" Section under Lieut Munro and 2/Lt Fell will advance from their present dugouts & consolidate the 1st objective in accordance with para 13

They will advance when an opportunity occurs, but must be in position by ZERO + 2 hrs

5/4/1917.

[signature] Barnett Lieut
for Major
Comdg No 44 M.G. Coy

Distribution

Copy No. 1 – O/C
2 – All officers
3 – War Diary
4 – File

SECRET OPERATION ORDER No 29 Copy No 8.

War Diary

BY MAJOR C KING

COMDG 44th M.G. COY. SUNDAY. 8th APRIL 1917

I The VI Corps will attack at ZERO on "Z" Day. The 15th Division will be in the centre with 12th Division on their right and the 9th Division on their left. The 37th Division are in reserve to the VI Corps.

II (1) The dividing line between the 12th and 15th Division

G30.b.2.8 — H25.b.6.8 — H26.a.6.6. — H28.c.8.2. — H35.a.5.8.

(2) The dividing line between the 15th and 9th Divisions, the R. SCARPE (Islands to 15th Division)

III The 15th Division will attack in accordance with Preliminary Instruction issued previously

IV The 7th Cameron Highrs and Machine Guns under 2/Lt Winn will leave their trenches at ZERO but will not pass the line of Trench Mortars about G24. c.3.2. before ZERO + 4 MINS.

2/Lt Winn will report at the 7th Cameron H.Qrs 3 hours before ZERO.

V At ZERO + 2 hours 20 mins the assaulting and Support Battns will advance against the BLUE LINE.

VI ZERO hour will be issued later, also arrangements for synchronising watches.

Issued at 2.0 P.M.

[illegible]

C King

Major

Comdg No 44 M.G. Coy.

Distribution

Copy No. 1 - O/C
2 - Lt. Munro
3 - 2/Lt Kell
4 - " Wenn
5 - " Cummins
6 - " Jenkins
7 } - War Diary
8 }

Copy

SECRET ADDENDUM No 1
TO · O.O No 29

1 (a) "Z" Day will be MONDAY
9th APRIL 1917.

(b) ZERO hour will be at 5.30 AM

This date & hour will not be mentioned to anyone whom it does not immediately concern.

Please acknowledge.

8/4/17

[signature]
Lieut
for Major
Comdg No 44 M.G. Coy

War Diary

SECRET ADDENDUM No. 2
TO O.O 29

The following officers will send a man with a reliable watch to meet 2/Lieut Schloss at Bde. H.Qrs at 1.30 AM 9/4/17.

Lieut Munro.
2/Lt. Fell.
" Winn.
" Jenkins.

8/4/17

[signature]
Lieut
for Major
Cmdg No. 44 M.G. Coy

Issued through Signals at 4.10 PM

SECRET OPERATIONS. 1917

SECOND PHASE.
Instruction No. 1

I At a date and hour to be notified later the 15th Division will attack from the front GOJEUL RIVER – N24 a. 0. 7 – LA BERGERE (inclusive).

1st Objective BLUE LINE.
Bridge at O.20. a. 3. 9½ up spur through O14 central – O. 8. C. and to small wood in O. 8. b. 5.6.

2nd Objective, RED LINE.
N. W corner of wood O 21. b. 3½. 0 – ST ROHART factory (inclusive) up spur through O. 15 central to road about O. 9. b 56.

II The Division will attack with 44th Inf Bde on right and 45th Inf Bde on the left.
Dividing line will be
BLUE Line Buildings etc in O. 14 a to 44 Inf Bde.
RED Line point of Spur about O. 15. b. 3. 4½

III The advance will be covered by a M.G. Barrage by 46th M.G. Coy under Divisional arrangements.

IV Proposals for attack.

IV. cont.

(a) 8th Seaforth Hrs will attack the village of GUEMAPPE, two Companies to advance directly against the village, one Coy to pass immediately to the North of the village in column of platoons, and turn south at its eastern end to block the exits & cover the flank of the 7th Cameron Hrs. One Company to be in Battalion Reserve.

2/Lt Jenkins with 2 guns (A Sect) will accompany 8th Seaforth Hrs advancing with the reserve company and consolidating when captured.

The attack will be supported by 2 guns (C Sect) under 2/Lt Schloss firing from about N.17. b.1.7 on houses in O.14.a and Sunken Road in O.13.c.

(b) 7th Cameron Hrs will advance with 2 Companies in front, each in 2 waves at 80 yds ~~in rear in similar formation~~ distance. The Support Coy 80 yds in rear in similar formation will follow the right Company. As soon as the second wave of the Support Coy is East of GUEMAPPE this Coy will turn half-right & move in echelon to the right rear of the leading Companies

IV (b) cont

As soon as 9th Black Watch occupy the Southern portion of the BLUE Line this Company can resume its original position.

The reserve Company will follow the left leading Company in artillery formation at a distance of 240 yds.

The battalion will occupy the BLUE Line and commence consolidation.

It will continue the attack to the RED Line from O.15.d.1.8 to the Northern boundary about O.15 b.1.4. They will consolidate their position when won.

2/Lt Cummings with 2 guns (D Sect) will accompany 7th Cameron Hrs advancing with the 2nd Support Wave throughout and finally consolidating on the RED Line.

C

9th Black Watch will leave the BROWN Line at ZERO in artillery formation & will follow 7th Cameron Hrs to the BLUE Line.

They will take over this line from river to O.14 C.7.8 and will advance to the RED Line with 7th Cameron Hrs.

IV. (C) Cont.
The dividing line between Battalion will be O.14 C.7.8 – O.15 C.2.8 – O.15.1.1.8. The Battalion will deploy into attack formation when the situation demands it, & in any case on reaching the BLUE Line.
2/Lt Marksman with 2 guns D Sect will accompany 9th Black Watch advancing to BLUE Line with Support Coy afterwards advancing to RED Line with 2nd Support wave.
d.
5/10th Gordon Hrs will follow 9th Black Watch into old BROWN Line & assembly trenches. 2 Companies will occupy & consolidate the BLUE LINE & 2 Companies will occupy the German trench running through N.18.b.
2/Lt Ground with 2 guns A Sect will accompany 5/10 Gordon Hrs & will consolidate near the old German Trench in N.18.b.

IV (e) cont.

Lt Munro with 4 guns (B Sect) will advance & cover consolidation of the BLUE LINE, by firing on the ST POHERT FACTORY and the bank in O. 14. d.
The guns being on a line N and S through N. 13 central.

(f) 2/Lt Wenn & 2/Lt Schloss with 4 guns (C Sect) will be in reserve.

V The advance from BLUE Line to RED Line will start at ZERO + 7 hours.

VI Kit will be carried as in "Preliminary Instruction"

VII

DUMPS	BRIGADE
A.R.A.	N. 16. d. 2. 2
A.R.B	N. 18. a. 6. 3
A.R.C	O. 14 C. 4. 8
A.R.D	O. 15. C. 5. 8

Mobile Dump G 35. a. 8. 8.

R.E
G. 29. a. 3. 2.

LT
Comdg No 44 MG Coy

SECRET OPERATIONS. 1917
2ND PHASE.
Instructions No. 2.

Ref. PARA I add.
The Southern boundary of the Division will now be the COJEUL RIVER. The Inter Brigade boundary will be from N.18.a.1.8 – O.14.a.9.5 – O.9.6.8.7.
Ref. Para IV (a) – for "the attack will be supported - - - - - - - - O.13.C"; read; The attack will be supported by four guns (C Sect) under Lieuts Wenn & Schaws firing on the area N of GUEMAPPE.
Cancel PARA IV (d) and insert. The 8/10th Gordon H[illegible]S will move into the BROWN LINE, 1 hour before ZERO; they will move forward when ordered by Brigade HQ.
2/Lt Groves with 2 guns "B" Sect will accompany this Battn, under orders of its C.O.
Ref. PARA IV(g) 8 guns (B & C Sects) will be active against targets to be detailed later, for 1 hour before ZERO to drown the noise of Tank movement.

(2)

Para VIII.

Units will be disposed as follows 1 hour before ZERO. The following trenches are referred to; their approximate positions are.

A ---- from N.18.c.4.½ to N.18.a.6.8

B --- from N.18.c.1.0 to N.18.a.2.8

C --- from N.17.b.8.0 to N.18.a.0.6.

8th Seaforth Hrs. Right half A & B trenches
H.Q. N.17.d.1.1.

7th Cameron Hrs. Left half A & B trenches. Whole of C trenches.
H.Q. N.11.a.5.2.

9th Black Watch – old front line.
H.Q. N.17.d.1.4.

8/10th Gordon Hrs. Old BROWN Line.
H.Q. N.16.b.1.8.

T.M. Battery. H.Q. N.11.a.5.2

M.G. Coy. H.Q. N.11.a.5.2.
'B' and 'C' Sects. Guns in position.
'A' and 'D' accomodated by respective Battns to which they are attached.
'B' and ½ 'C' Sects H.Q. at N.11.d.1.6.
4LT. [illegible] H.Q. N.16.a.9.7.

(3)

PARA IX. – The artillery Barrage will lift at the rate of 100 yds in 4 minutes.

PARA X.

There is a 3rd objective, the GREEN line, which runs, O.34 central – Brickworks. – O.29.c – O.29.a.3.3 – O.23.c.6.9 – O.17.a.8.9 – O.11. Central – O.5.d.5.0 – I.35.d.5.0.

This line will not be attacked on the same day as the RED and BLUE lines.

[signature]

Cmdg No 44 M.G. Coy

21/6/17

SECRET OPERATION ORDER NO [illegible] Copy 7
War Diary

by Lt [illegible] Barrett
Comdg No [illegible] M.G. Coy

i [illegible] M.G. Coy will take over night [illegible] [illegible] M.G. Coy on night [illegible].

ii Guns will be distributed as follows:–

2 guns	N. 11 [illegible]	— C	Section
2	N. 11. [illegible]. 6. 2.	— B	"
2	N. 17. [illegible]. 1. 7.	— B	

iii Lt [illegible] will be i/c [illegible] guns [illegible] Sgt Schloss will be i/c 2 guns [illegible]

iv All teams will consist of [illegible] men who will take with them gun, [illegible], 2 cans water, 2 belt boxes, 2 days Rations.

v [illegible] and [illegible] will be handed over at each gun position.

vi The remainder of the Company will remain in cellars. R[illegible] of DOUAI.

vii Coy H.Q. will be at N. [illegible].

viii Guides 1 per gun will meet Coy at new Coy H.Q. at 7.30 PM.

ix The Coy will march off from billets at [illegible] PM.

x The following route will be followed. ARRAS STATION [illegible] TILLOY — WANCOURT.

[illegible signature] Barrett
Lt
Comdg No [illegible] M.G. Coy

DISTRIBUTION

Copy No 1 – O/C
2 – Lt [illegible]
3 – " Rogers
4 – Sgt Schloss.
5 – C.S.M.
6 – War Diary
7 – "

SECRET Operation Order No. 21
by Lieut K.V. Barrett
Comdg No 44 M.G. Coy
25th. 4 - 1917

I 44th Inf Bde will relieve Right half of 46th Inf Bde from CAMBRAI ROAD (inclusive) to RIVER COJEUL

II The 16 guns of the Company will be disposed as follows.

Guns	Sect	Officer	Position	Object and direction of fire
2 4	A C	Winn Schlon	N.18.d.0.7	Defensive Barrage on GRID between O.14 and O.15
2 1 1	A D B	Jenkins	N.19.a	Defence O.14. C
2	B	Munro	O.13.d.8.8	at disposal of 9th Black Watch.
2	D	Cumming	N.13.d.9.4	at disposal of 7 Cameron Hrs
1 1	B D	C.S. Major	N.16.a.8½.9	out of action
Headquarters			N 18 C.2.4	
Brigade H.Q			N 16.b.1.9	

III.- Lieuts Winn, Schlon and Jenkins will be in position by midnight 25/26. Lieuts Munro and Cumming to proceed to their positions with their respective battalions

O.O 31 (cont) (2)

IV Sgt Caddick will detail runners for Lieut's Munro & Cumming

V The 2 teams at present under Sgt Richardson with the 8/10 Gordon H'rs, will withdraw to N 18 d 0.7 where they will replace 2 teams of B' Sect, who will be advancing with Lieut Munro.

VI A store of belt boxes and water will be made at N 16 a 8½ 9 under C.S.M.
This will be the rationing point (after 6 PM daily) water cans (full) can be exchanged for water cans (empty)

R B[arnett]

Lieut

Comdg No 44 MG Coy

SECRET Operation Order No. 32.
By Lieut K.V. Barrett.
Comdg No 44 M.G. Coy

I The 44th M.G. Coy will be relieved by the 167th M.G. Coy. on night 28/29 April 1917.

II The following guns will be relieved, the remainder being withdrawn.
4 guns in N.24.b., 2 guns in N.18.c.
2 " " O.13.b.

III GUIDES: 4 guides will be at 45 M.G.Coy H.Q. at 3.0PM to guide incoming teams to 44th M.G.Coy H.Q. at N.18.c.2.5.

IV On relief teams will return to Coy H.Q.

V Lts Winn & Schloss will withdraw their remaining guns on relief.

VI Lt. Munro will withdraw at 9.0PM.

VII TRANSPORT:- 1 limber for H.Q. to be at H.Q. N.18.a.2.5 at 5.0PM. It will pick up Munro's load at Concrete emplacement N.16.a.9½.8, on its way back. 1 limber for 4 guns "C" Sect, 2 guns A Sect at N.18.a.2.5 at 4.0PM.
1. Limber for 2 guns "A" 2 guns "B", & 2 guns "D" at N.18.a.2.5. at 4.30PM. They will pick up one gun "A" and 1 gun "D" at N.16.a.9½.8
1 limber for 2 guns "B" 2 guns "D" at N.18.a.2.5 at 10.0PM.

VIII On relief parties will move direct to Rue de Douai ARRAS with limbers. Limbers to go on to transport lines.

IX Lt Cumming will hand over 8 belt boxes per gun in good condition.

K.V. Barrett. Lt
Comdg No 44th M.G.Coy

SECRET

Operation Order No 33
by Lt. K.V. Barrett
Comdg No 44 MG Coy

I 44th Inf Bde will move to SIMENCOURT on 29th April.

II ROUTE – RUE D'AMIENS – DAINVILLE – BERNEVILLE.

III Lieut Schlom & 4 Signallers to report for billeting to Town Major at 12 NOON.

IV Advance Party: Officers mess & Company cooks with Lt Jenkins to be clear of ARRAS by 3.0 PM.

V PARADES:

Sectional Inspection 2.45 PM
Coy move off 3.0 "
Pass starting point 4.0 P.

K Barrett
Lt
Comdg No 44 MG Coy

Instructions regarding War Diaries and Intelligence Summaries are contained in F. S. Regs., Part II. and the Staff Manual respectively. Title pages will be prepared in manuscript.

WAR DIARY
or
INTELLIGENCE SUMMARY.
(*Erase heading not required.*)

Army Form C. 2118.

Vol 15

Place	Date	Hour	Summary of Events and Information	Remarks and references to Appendices
			CONFIDENTIAL	
			War Diary	
			of the	
			44th Machine Gun Company	
			from 1st May 1917 to 31st May 1917	
			(Volume XVI)	
			K Barrett Capt	

A5834 Wt. W4973/M687 750,000 8/16 D. D. & L. Ltd. Forms/C.2118/13.

Instructions regarding War Diaries and Intelligence Summaries are contained in F. S. Regs., Part II. and the Staff Manual respectively. Title pages will be prepared in manuscript.

WAR DIARY
or
INTELLIGENCE SUMMARY.

(Erase heading not required.)

Army Form C. 2118.

Place	Date	Hour	Summary of Events and Information	Remarks and references to Appendices
SIMENCOURT	1/5/17		Training at SIMENCOURT. Programme attached. Lieut. R. WILSON reported for duty from Base Depôt	LSW Ref LENS 1/100.000 H3 9.2
"	2/5/17		Training as per programme. Nothing to report.	LSW
	3/5/17		Training as per programme	LSW
	4/5/17		Training as per programme	LSW
	5/5/17		Training as per programme	LSW
	6/5/17		Training as per programme 2/Lt. MARSHALL reported for duty from Base Depôt	LSW
	7/5/17		Training as per programme	LSW
	8/5/17		Moved with Brigade to SOMBRIN. Operation order attached.	LSW Ref LENS 1/100.000 F4 0.9
SOMBRIN	9/5/17		Training at SOMBRIN.	LSW
"	10/5/17		Training at SOMBRIN – programme attached.	LSW
	11/5/17		Training as per programme	LSW
	12/5/17		Training " "	LSW
	13/5/17		Training " "	LSW
	14/5/17		Training " "	LSW
	15/5/17		Training " "	LSW
	16/5/17		Training " "	LSW
	17/5/17		Training " "	LSW
	18/5/17		Training " "	LSW
	19/5/17		Training " "	LSW
	20/5/17		Training " "	LSW
	21/5/17		~~Training~~ Moved to BOURET. Operation order attached	LSW Ref LENS 1/100.000 D3 9.2

[illegible] Capt

A5834 Wt. W4973/M687 750,000 8/16 D. D. & L. Ltd. Forms/C.2118/13.

Instructions regarding War Diaries and Intelligence Summaries are contained in F. S. Regs., Part II. and the Staff Manual respectively. Title pages will be prepared in manuscript.

WAR DIARY
~~or~~
~~INTELLIGENCE SUMMARY.~~
(Erase heading not required.)

Army Form C. 2118.

Place	Date	Hour	Summary of Events and Information	Remarks and references to Appendices
FRESNOY	22/5/17		Moved to FRESNOY. Operation order attached.	LSW R4 LENS 1/100 000
	23/5/17		Training at FRESNOY Programme attached.	LSW B2 25
	24/5/17		Training. 2/Lt BOWN reported for duty	LSW
	25/5/17		Training as per programme	LSW
	26/5/17		Training as per programme	LSW
	27/5/17		Training. Lieut BARRETT promoted Captain to command the Company dated 26/4/17	LSW
	28/5/17		Training as per programme	LSW
	29/5/17		Training as per programme	LSW
	30/5/17		Practice for proposed inspection by French General.	LSW
	31/5/17		Training at FRESNOY	LSW

(Volume XVI)

[signature] Barrett Capt
Cand 44 M.G. Company

A5834 Wt. W4973/M687 750,000 8/16 D. D. & L. Ltd. Forms/C.2118/13.

SECRET OPERATION ORDER No. 34
by Lieut K.V. Barrett.
Comdg No 44 M.G. Coy

I The 44th M.G. Coy will move to SOMBRIN on 8/ May 1917.

II There will be a two hours halt for dinner in the wood in P20 and 26 S of BARLY.

III Transport will be brigaded with exception of Cooks Cart, mess cart & Water Cart which will accompany unit

IV A billeting party, Lieuts Jenkins and Fell, Sgt Caddick & four Signallers and a Transport N.C.O will report to Town Major SOMBRIN at 10. A.M.

V Lieut Wenn will report to Bde Major at 8.A.M at the starting point to synchronize watches.

VI Brigade H.Q. will open at GRAND ROLLECOURT at 1.0 P.M.

VII Starting point will be Cross Roads W of SIMENCOURT Q.10.c.6.9.

O.O. 34 (cont)

VIII. Company will pass starting point at 9.17 AM.

IX PARADES:-

6.0 AM Reveille
7.0 " Breakfasts
by 8.0 " Blankets to be on limbers.
8.45 " Section Inspection
9.0 " Coy marches off from billets.

X DRESS:-
Marching order. Packs and greatcoats.

J Barrett
Lieut
Comdg No 44 M.G. Coy

SECRET War Diary

OPERATION ORDER Nº 35.

by Lieut K.V. Barrett

Comdg 44th M.G. Coy. 20/5/17

I The 44th M.G. Coy will move to BOURET via ETREE WAMIN & REBREUVETTE, on 21st May 1917.

II Transport will move with the Company.

III A billeting party, Lieut Jenkins, Interpreter, Sgt Caddick & 4 Signallers will report to Town Major BOURET at 7.0 AM.

IV The Company will pass the Starting point (O.9.a.3.9) the junction of LE CAUROY – GD RULLECOURT & HENCOURT – GD RULLECOURT roads at 6.47 AM

V 2/Lt Schloss will meet the Bdge Major at the Starting point at 6.0AM to Synchronize watches.

VI Bde H.Q will be at REBREUVE.

VII PARADES.

3.45 AM Reveille

4.15 " Blankets on limber.

4.30 " Breakfasts.

5.35 " Coy Parade

5.50 " Coy Move Off

K.V. Barrett

Lieut

Comdg 44 M.G. Coy

War Diary

SECRET OPERATION ORDER No. 36
by Lieut K. V. Barrett
Comdg 44th M.G. Coy. 21st 5 17

I The 44th M.G. Coy will move to WAIL on 22nd May 1917.

II A billeting party, 2/Lt Jenkins, Interpreter, Sgt Caddick & 4 Signallers will report to the MAIRE; WAIL at 8.30AM.

III The Company will pass the starting point, - Cross roads in BOUBERS SUR CANCHES at 9.2AM.

IV The Road junction at FREVENT Church in the centre of town to be clear of troops by 9.0AM, and VACQUERIE LE BOUCQ by 8.0AM.

V Bde H.Q. will close at 7.0AM at HONVAL and open again in WAIL.

VI PARADES:-

5.0AM Reveille
5.30. Blankets on limber.
5.45. Breakfasts.
6.45. Coy. Parade
7.0. Coy move off.

G. Jenkins for Lieut
Comdg 44 MG Coy.

1	2	3	4	5	7	6th
9 am Section Inspection 9-30-10.30 Gun Drill 10.45-11.30 Squad Drill 11.30-12.30 Withdrawal of Winter Clothing	8.45 Section Inspect 9-10 Squad Drill 10-10.45 Indication & Recognition of Targets 11-12 Gun Drill 12-12.30 I A	6.45-7.15 P.T. 8.45 Section Inspection 9-10 T.O.E.T. 10-10.30 Indication & Recognition 10.30-11 Fire Orders 11.15-12.30 Advanced Drill	6.45-7.15 P.T. 8.45 Section Inspection 9-12.30 Range 2-3 Squad Drill	6.45-7.15 P.T. 8.45 Section Inspect 9-12.30 Range 2-3 Squad Drill	6.45-7.15 P.T. 8.45 Section Inspect. 9-12.30 Range 2-3 Cover Drill	Sunday. Church Parades

[illegible] Capt
Cmdg 441 M.G. Coy.

8	9	10	11	12	14	13
More to SOMBRIN	6.45 - 7.15 1 A	645 - 7.15 1A	645 7.15 1 A	645 - 7.15 1A	645 - 7.15 IA	Church Parades
	8.45 Section Inspect.	8.45 Sectional Inspection	8.45 Section Inspect	8.45 Section Insp.	8.45 Section Insp.	
	9 - 10.30 Inspection of Box Respirators	9 - 1.0 Range	9 - 1.0 Range	9.0 - 11 Tactical Scheme	9 - 1 Range Each Section does 2 hrs Range and then Gun Drill, P.T. & Cleaning Guns	
	11 - 11.30 P.T.			11 - 11.45 P.T.		
	12 - 12.30 Mechanism	When not actually on Range, Sections do Advanced Drill, Gun Drill & P.T.		12 - 12.30 Pouls. B.D.A		Sunday

[signature] Capt
Cmdg 44th M.G. Coy

15	16	17	18	19	20
Brigade Tactical Scheme	6.45 - 7.15 1A 8.45 Section Inspection 9 - 1 Range. Two hours per Section. Remaining two hours Gun Drill P.T. & Cleaning Guns.	6.45 - 7.15 1A 8.45 Section Inspection. 9 - 1 Same as for 16th inst.	6.45 - 7.15 1A 8.45 Section Inspection 8.30 - 12 A+B Range 2 - 3 Gun Drill 9 - 10 C+D Range 10.30 - 3 Range	6.45 - 7.15 1A 8.45 Section Inspection 9 - 1 Range Each Section two hours. Remaining two hours - Gun Drill P.T. Squad Drill	Sunday Church Parades night of 21 - 22nd Move to FRESNOY via BEURET

[signature] Capt
Cmd 144 M/G Coy

23	24	25	26	28	29	27
6.45 – 7.15 1 A 8.45 Section Inspection 9 – 10 Cleaning & Overhauling 10 – 10.45 Gun Drill 11 – 11.30 P.T. 11.45 – 12.30 Overhead Fire 12.30 – 1 Squad Drill	6.45 – 7.15 1 A 9 – 10 Gun Drill 12 – 4 pm Range. 30th. Preparation for Inspection by French General	6.45 7.15 1 A 8.45 Section Inspection 9 – 12 A Section Range 12 – 12.30 Cleaning guns 1.45 – 3 D & C Section Range B Section Tactical Scheme	6.45 – 7.15 1 A 8.45 Section Inspection 9 – 1 Range for two hours. Gun Drill PT & Squad Drill — each Section	6.45 – 7.15 1 A 8.45 Section Inspection 9 – 1 Each Section two hours on Revolver range. Two hours Gun Drill P.T.	~~Parade for Inspection~~ 6.45 7.15 1 A 8.45 Section Inspection 8 – 12 A & B Sections Range 9 4 – 2 C & D Sections Range	Sunday Church Parades 31st 9 – 11.30 Advanced Drill 11.45 – 12.15 Characteristics 12.30 – 1 Company Drill

[illegible signature]
Capt
Cmdg 44 M.G. Coy

Instructions regarding War Diaries and Intelligence Summaries are contained in F. S. Regs., Part II. and the Staff Manual respectively. Title pages will be prepared in manuscript.

WAR DIARY
or
~~INTELLIGENCE SUMMARY.~~

(Erase heading not required.)

Army Form C. 2118.

Vol 16

Place	Date	Hour	Summary of Events and Information	Remarks and references to Appendices
			Confidential WAR DIARY OF 44th MACHINE GUN COY from 1st June 1917 to 30th June 1917 (Volume XVII) J Barrett Capt Comd) 44 M.G. Coy	

A5834 Wt. W4973/M687 750,000 8/16 D. D. & L. Ltd. Forms/C.2118/13.

Army Form C. 2118.

Instructions regarding War Diaries and Intelligence Summaries are contained in F. S. Regs., Part II. and the Staff Manual respectively. Title pages will be prepared in manuscript.

WAR DIARY

~~or~~

~~INTELLIGENCE SUMMARY.~~

(Erase heading not required.)

Place	Date	Hour	Summary of Events and Information	Remarks and references to Appendices
FRESNOY	1/6/17		Training at FRESNOY Ref LENS 11. 1/100 000	
	2/6/17		Training at FRESNOY B 2. 50. 50	L.SH
	3/6/17		Training at FRESNOY	
	4/6/17		Training at FRESNOY	
	5/6/17		Training at FRESNOY	L.SH
	6/6/17		Inspection by G.O.C. XVth Division	
	7/6/17		Training at FRESNOY	L.SH
	8/6/17		Training at FRESNOY	
	9/6/17		Brigade operation	
	10/6/17		Training at FRESNOY	L.SH
	11/6/17		Training	
	12/6/17		Training	
	13/6/17		Training	
	14/6/17		Training	
	15/6/17		Training	
	16/6/17		Training	
	17/6/17		Training	
	18/6/17		Training. Brigade Operation	
	19/6/17		Training	
	20/6/17		Company moved to SIRACOURT Operation Order attached Ref LENS. 11. 1/100 000	L.SH
SIRACOURT	21/6/17		Company moved to ANTIN. Operation Order attached D. 2. 20. 50	L.SH
ANTIN	22/6/17		Ref LENS 11 1/100 000 E1 50. 10	

A5834 Wt. W4973/M687 750,000 8/16 D. D. & L. Ltd. Forms/C.2118/13.

Army Form C. 2118.

WAR DIARY

or

~~INTELLIGENCE SUMMARY~~.

(Erase heading not required.)

Instructions regarding War Diaries and Intelligence Summaries are contained in F. S. Regs., Part II. and the Staff Manual respectively. Title pages will be prepared in manuscript.

Place	Date	Hour	Summary of Events and Information	Remarks and references to Appendices
LESPESSES	23/6/17		Company moved to LESPESSES. Operation order attached Ref. [illegible] 1/100 000 HAZEBROUCK F6 10.50	LSW
"	24/6/17		Resting and cleaning	LSW
THIENNES	25/6/17		Moved to THIENNES. Operation order attached " F5 70.5	LSW
CAESTRE	26/6/17		Coy moved to CAESTRE Operation order attached 4 3 20.15	LSW
BRANDHOEK	27/6/17		Coy moved to BRANDHOEK Operation order attached	LSW
"	28/6/17		Resting & cleaning	LSW
"	29/6/17		Relieved 46 M G Coy in the line in front of YPRES Operation order attached	LSW
"	30/6/17		Nothing to report	

A5834 Wt. W4973/M687 750,000 8/16 D. D. & L. Ltd. Forms/C.2118/13.

SECRET . OPERATION ORDER. No 37
by Capt K.V. Barrett
Comdg 44th M.G. Coy
21.6.1917

I 44th M.G. Coy will move to SIRACOURT (via OEUF & road junction 1 mile W of R in RAMECOURT) on 21st June 1917.

II The Company will pass the starting point, the 4 cross roads 200 yds N.W. of W in WILLEMAN at 4.37 AM.

III Transport to accompany unit.

IV Billeting party consisting of L/Cpl Munro Sgt Caddick & 4 Signallers to obtain billets from the MAIRIE SIRACOURT. They will leave FRESNOY at 3.45 AM.

V Brigade H.Q. will be at CROIX.

VI PARADES

2.0 AM Reveille
2.30 " Breakfast.
3.45 " Parade
4.0 — March off.

DRESS: Fighting order with steel helmets carried on top of mess tin. F.S. Caps to be worn.

J.V. Barrett
Capt.
Comdg 44th M.G. Coy.

Secret

Operation Order No 38
by Capt R V Barrett
Cmdg 44 M.G. Coy
22 June 1917

i The 44th MG Coy will move to VALHUON via CROIX, ST POL on 22 June

ii The Coy will pass the starting point Road junction 300 yards E of last . E of FAUB de BETHUNE (NE of ST POL.) at 6.0 AM

iii Brigade H.Q will be at PERNES

iv PARADES:
2.0 AM Reveille
2.30 Breakfast
4.0 Coy Parade

[signature]
Capt
Cmdg 44 M.G. Coy

Secret Operation Order No 39
by Capt K.V. Barrett
Comdg 44 M.G. Coy.

i The 44 M.G. Coy will move to LESSPRESSES (via Ferfay 4 X roads 400 yds N of Y in BELLERY - LILLERS Road junction 600 yds W of L in LESPRESSES) on 28/6/17

ii The Company will pass the starting point 4 cross roads 300 yds N of Y in CAUCHY-A-LA-TOUR at 11.19 AM.

iii PARADES:-

6.30 AM Reveille
7.15 " Breakfasts
8.45 " Coy. Parade

KV Barrett
Capt
Comdg 44 M.G. Coy

Operation Order No 40
by Capt K. V. Barrett
Comdg 44 MG Coy

I The 44 MG Coy will move to THIENNES on the 25th June 1917.

II Usual billeting party will report to Staff Captain at THIENNES.

III PARADES.

5.30 AM Reveille
6.0 " Breakfasts
7.15 " Company March off.

K V Barrett
Capt
Comdg 44 MG Coy

Operation Order No. 41
by Capt K V Barrett
Comdg 44 M.G. Coy

I The 44 M.G. Coy will move from THIENNES to CAESTRE via HAZEBROUCKE on the 26th June 1917.

II PARADES

1.30 AM Reveille
2.0 Breakfasts
3.15 Company March off.

K V Barrett

Captain
Comdg 44 M.G. Coy

Operation Order No 42.
by Capt K. V. Barrett
Comdg 44th M.G. Coy

i The 44th M.G. Coy will move from CAESTRE to TORONTO CAMP POPERINGHE on the 27th June 1917

ii The usual billeting party will report to 15th Division H.Q. "A" by 6.30 AM.

iii PARADES:

3.0 AM Reveille
3.30 " Breakfasts
4.0 " Company March off.

A & B Sections will join Company at the Church CAESTRE.

[signature]

Capt
Comdg 44 M.G. Coy

Secret. Copy

OPERATION ORDER No 43.

by Capt K.V. Barrett.

Comdg 44 M.G. Coy. — 29th 6.1917.

I. The 44 M.G. Coy will relieve the 46th M.G. Coy on the night 29/30 June.

II. Guides 1 per Section at the REIGERSBURG CHATEAU at 10.0 PM to guide to SCHOOL HOUSE thence 1 per gun team.

III. DISTRIBUTION:-

2/Lt Jenkins & 2/Lt Wilson.
H.Q I.6.a.10.75 MILL COT
No 1 Team } I.6.a.10.75.
No 2 "

Lieut Munro
H.Q I.4.d.15.70
No 5 team I.5.c.55.10 GOLLY TR
No 6 " I.1.a.30.87 JULY SWITCH.
No 7 " I.5.b.30.20 DILLY FARM
No 8 " I.4.d.15.70 JAMES FARM.

2/Lt Bass. H.Q as for Lt Munro
No 13 team I.11.a.95.30 EAST LANE.
" 14 " I.10.d.50.90 WEST "
" 15 " I.10.a.70.30 EAST "
" 16 " I.4.d.15.70 PICCADILLY

Nos 3, 4, 9, 10, 11 & 12 teams will be at SCHOOL HOUSE.

H.Q at SCHOOL HOUSE I.9.c.2.0.

IV. 10 belt boxes per gun will be taken over. 8 at each position & 80 at SCHOOL HOUSE.

V. The Coy will march up by Sections at 300 yds interval via VLAMERTINGE (VLAMERTINGE - BRIELEN Road) – HIGH STREET. Sgt Caddick will arrange for the necessary connecting files.

VI. The Coy will leave Camp at 8.15 PM.

VII. Transport. — A & B Sects will pack gun kit on one limber
C & D " " " " " " "
no belt boxes will be taken.

1 limber will be for H.Q mess & officers packs. ~~Water cart will accompany.~~

VIII. 44th M.G. Coy will be under the orders of 46th Bde until 9 AM 1st July.

IX. No 15 of 46th M.G. Coy teams will be in the line for 24 hours. The will be relieved by the 10 teams in the line.

K Barrett

Captain

Comdg 44 M.G. Coy

Instructions regarding War Diaries and Intelligence Summaries are contained in F. S. Regs., Part II. and the Staff Manual respectively. Title pages will be prepared in manuscript.

WAR DIARY
or
INTELLIGENCE SUMMARY.
(Erase heading not required.)

Vol. 17

Army Form C. 2118.

Place	Date	Hour	Summary of Events and Information	Remarks and references to Appendices
			CONFIDENTIAL WAR DIARY of 44th Machine Gun Coy from 1st July 1917 to 31st July 1917 VOLUME XVIII (ORIGINAL)	

A5834 Wt. W4973/M687 750,000 8/16 D. D. & L. Ltd. Forms/C.2118/13.

Instructions regarding War Diaries and Intelligence Summaries are contained in F. S. Regs., Part II. and the Staff Manual respectively. Title pages will be prepared in manuscript.

WAR DIARY

~~or~~

~~INTELLIGENCE SUMMARY.~~

(*Erase heading not required.*)

Army Form C. 2118.

Place	Date	Hour	Summary of Events and Information	Remarks and references to Appendices
Toronto Camp BRANDHOEK	1/7/17		Nothing to report	LSW
	2/7/17		Nothing to report	
	3/7/17		Indirect fire carried out on enemy communications	LSW
	4/7/17		Indirect fire carried out on enemy communications	LSW
	5/7/17		Indirect fire	LSW
	6/7/17		Indirect fire	LSW
	7/7/17		Raid by 8th Seaforth Highlanders Machine Gun box barrage on sector raided	LSW
	8/7/17		44 Machine Gun Company relieved by 45th Machine Gun Company. Operation order attached.	LSW
	9.7.17		Training at Toronto Camp	LSW
	10.7.17		Brigade entrained at POPERINGHE for ROUBROUCK	LSW
ROBROUCK	11.7.17		Training at ROBROUCK.	LSW
	12/7.17		Training at ROBROUCK	LSW
	13.7.17		Training at ROBROUCK	LSW
	14.7.17		Brigade Tactical Scheme.	LSW
	15.7.17		Training	LSW
	16.7.17		Brigade Tactical Scheme	LSW
	17.7.17		Right half Company under Capt BARRETT moved to WORMHOUDT.	LSW
TORONTO Camp	18.7.17		Right half Company moved to TORONTO Camp	LSW
	19.7.17		Right half Company ~~moved~~ relieved half of 45 Machine Gun Company Operation order attached.	LSW

A5834 Wt. W4973/M687 750,000 8/16 D. D. & L. Ltd. Forms/C.2118/13.

Instructions regarding War Diaries and Intelligence Summaries are contained in F. S. Regs., Part II. and the Staff Manual respectively. Title pages will be prepared in manuscript.

WAR DIARY
or
~~INTELLIGENCE SUMMARY~~.
(Erase heading not required.)

Army Form C. 2118.

Place	Date	Hour	Summary of Events and Information	Remarks and references to Appendices
YPRES	20.7.7		Nothing to report	LSh
	21.7.7		Left half Coy moved from ROBROUCK. Operation order attached	LSh
	22.7.7		Left half Coy moved to WATTEAU. 4 guns of 225 (Divisional) Machine Gun Coy relieved 4 guns of this Coy	LSh
TORONTO CAMP	23.7.7		Left half Coy moved to TORONTO CAMP	LSh
YPRES	24.7.7		Nothing to report	LSh
	25.7.7		Raid by N.F.l. – 70 prisoners. Patrol of 7th Cameron Hdrs captured Machine Gun	LSh
	26.7.7		Nothing to report	LSh
	27.7.7		Nothing to report	LSh
	28.7.7		Raid by 7th Cameron Hdrs 2 officers + 50 OR prisoners	LSh
	29.7.7		Nothing to report.	LSh
	30.7.7		Nothing to report	
	31.7.7		Zero day. The 15 Div attacked the enemy positions in front of YPRES. Blue, Black & Green lines captured, but subsequently retired from Green line. Preliminary instructions carried out. 2/Lts SCHLOSS & BROWN killed.	LSh

A5834 Wt. W4973/M687 750,000 8/16 D. D. & L. Ltd. Forms/C.2118/13.

War Diary

SECRET

Copy [illegible]

YPRES - 1917.

Preliminary Instructions by Captain K. V. BARRETT Commanding 44th MACHINE GUN COMPANY.

GENERAL

1. The offensive in Belgium will be resumed at a date to be notified later.

15th Division will assault with 44th Infantry Brigade on the Right, 46th Infantry Brigade on the left, 45th Infantry Brigade will be in reserve.

2. There are three objectives shown approximately on attached map –

(1) The BLUE line.

(2) The BLACK line

(3) The GREEN line

The 44th and 46th Brigades will capture and consolidate the BLUE and BLACK lines. 45th Brigade will capture and consolidate the GREEN line. There will be a halt of half an hour on the BLUE line and of four hours on the BLACK line.

3. The 15th and 16th Divisional Artilleries and two Army Brigades R.F.A will co-operate, covering the assault with a creeping shrapnel barrage which will advance at the rate of 100 yards in four minutes.

4. Two Sections of Tanks will assist 44th Infantry Brigade in the capture of BLACK line.

5. The advance to the BLACK line will be covered by an indirect Machine Gun Barrage.

6. 44th Brigade will attack [illegible]

[illegible]

[illegible]

The assaulting Battalions will capture the BLUE and BLACK lines and will consolidate the latter.

[illegible] Line will be occupied by the Support Battalion as soon as vacated by the leading Battalions.

7/ The Boundaries of the Brigade front of attack are as ~~[illegible]~~ in attached map & shown thus:-

Divisional Boundary ———

Brigade Boundary ———

8/ (a) The assaulting Battalions will each attack on a front of two Companies, each company on a front of two platoons, one Company in support, one Company in reserve. Vickers Guns will accompany the Reserve Company.

(b). The support Battalion will follow the assaulting Battalions across "NO MAN'S LAND" and will in the first instance occupy the front German Trench System.

9/ 44 M.G. Coy. 8 guns will be employed in the first instance under the orders of D.M.G.O. for indirect barrage.

2 guns will be attached to each of of the three leading Battalions.

2 guns will be in reserve.

10/ A chain of dumps will be established on the relay system.

A mobile dump of pack animals will also be formed and will be available to push as far forward as the situation admits.

The following works will be carried out under the C.R.E's orders.

(c). Open up the Potizje – Zonnebeke Road.

EMPLOYMENT of R.E.

making it fit for Artillery and limbered wagons.

(b) Open up two tracks wide enough for guns and horsed transport. Shown on attached map thus:-

(c). Build strong points at:-

1) D 26 a 7.2.

2) D 20 c 7.2.

3) D 20 a 5.9.

Shown on attached map thus:-

CONSOLIDATION

The consolidation of the objectives will be commenced by the construction of a chain of strong points.

The BLUE line will contain five of these situated approximately as follows:-

(a). J. 1. a ½. 3.
(b). I. 6 B. 8½. 6.
(c). I. 6 B. 6. 7.
(d). I. 6 B. 3. 9.
(e). I. 6 B. ½. 9½.

Shown on attached map thus:-

These posts will be constructed by the Reserve Battalion. The two Reserve Machine Guns under Lt. JENKINS will move to this line. Post (c) will probably be the most suitable position for them.

The BLACK line will contain five strong points approximately as follows:-

(a). J. 1. b. 2. 9.
(b). D. 25. d. 1. 2.
(c). D. 25. d. ½. 4½.
(d). D. 25. c. 9. 6½.
(e). D. 25. c. 8½. 9.

Shown on attached map thus:-

The two Machine Guns attached to the

Support Battalion under 2/Lt. MARSHALL will be posted in Post D.

The Machine Guns attached to the assaulting Battalions will be distributed among the other four posts.

[illegible] OF SURPLUS PERSONNEL.

The following will be surplus personnel and will be accomodated at TORONTO CAMP (Except Transport who will act under orders of Brigade Transport Officer.

LIEUT. ROGERS.
" MUNRO.
2/Lt. CUMMING.
TRANSPORT. approximately 35 other Ranks.
C.Q.M.S.
Cpl. WINSOR.
Sgt. HARRIS.
L/Cpl. GREENLAND.
" McClelland.
Pte. SPARES.
" [illegible]
" [illegible]
" SPIERS.
" LANE. }
" ROBSON } To be attached to Mobile Dump as Pack Pony Leaders.
" YATES. }
Cpl. MORRISON. N.C.O. with Mobile Dump Party.
L/Cpl. Mc.ARTHUR. Post Corporal.

[illegible] MOVEMENTS.

Collecting Posts will be on the Potijze and Menin Roads at I.4.a.7.2 and at I.9.b.[illegible] as shown on attached tracing.

Walking Wounded. The route will be clearly marked out by sign-boards by the new route round the South of Ypres, via KRUISSTRAAT to the VLAMER

M.D.S. [illegible] wounded [illegible] Station.

There will be a Soup Kitchen [illegible] at [illegible] for [illegible]

The Divisional [illegible] Dressing Station will be at BRANDHOEK [illegible]

DUMPS

The 44th Infantry Brigade dumps will be as follows:

B.A.A.	Brigade dump	[illegible] 1.A.6.7½
A.S.D.	(Rations).	[illegible] 6.5.
A.R.D.		[illegible] (THATCH BARN).
A.A.C.		About [illegible] 9.7.
A.R.D.		About [illegible]

[illegible]

A.R ?

ORGANISATION of MOBILE DUMP

Ration Section. Total [illegible] animals. Divided into 4 Sections each of 13 animals carrying:-

5. Water.
6 Rations.
1. Spare.

} Approximately [illegible]

Machine Gun Company and Trench Mortar Battery to be rationed by Units in whose area they may be.

Explosive Section. Total 52 animals. Divided into 4 Sections.

Total carried by Explosive Section.

40 Boxes S.A.A.

50 " STOKES.

60 " No.23 Rifle Grenades.

100 " No 5 Mills Bombs.

32 " FLARES and LIGHTS.

Each Battalion to furnish 13 animals. M.G. Coy to furnish 8 animals – Total 100 Animals.

[illegible] ARRANGEMENTS.

From Z day inclusive an Advanced Collecting Post & Dressing Station will be established near VLAMERTINGHE at [illegible] Central.

No 27 Mobile Veterinary Section will remain at Camp [illegible] and [illegible]

DRESS & EQUIPMENT.

FIGHTING KIT.

STEEL HELMET.

EQUIPMENT. (a) Entrenching Tool and Carrier.

(b) Haversack carried on the back.

(c) Respirator and P.H. HELMET.

(d) Mess Tin and 1 Water Bottle.

(e) Waterproof Sheet.

(f) Rations for Z and Z plus 1 days and the Emergency Ration.

The following will also be carried.

100 Rounds S.A.A. per Vickers Gunner.

5 Sandbags per man.

Teams will each carry:-

Gun.
Tripod.
Condenser.
1st Aid Case.
2 Cans Water.
10 Belt Boxes.
1 Pick and 2 Shovels.

PRISONERS of WAR.

Will be handed over to Infantry Escorts.

DIRECTION of TRAFFIC.

1) Traffic Routes for Transport Vehicles after Zero hour until further orders will be as follows:-

Forward – from vicinity H.17.D.

(a) KRUISSTRAAT – MENIN GATE to { HELLFIRE CORNER { (i) to Potijze or (ii) I.17.b.25.80. } CAMBRIDGE Rd TRACKS

(b) H.18.d.6.2. – WARRINGTON ROAD (wooden) – BRIDGE No.1. (I.13.d.0.2.) – LILLE GATE – thence via GORDON TRACK to I.9.d. Central.

__Return.__ POTIJZE – YPRES – (This may be used as a forward road for clearing existing dumps).

2) No vehicle will halt on the YPRES – POTIJZE Road, but will draw off the road if a halt is required.

3) __Communication Trenches__

__UP.__ PICCADILLY.
HAYMARKET.

__DOWN.__ EAST and WEST LANES
CURZON

7.

COMMUNICATIONS. Approximate route for Cable and runners:-

(a) At ZERO – at dug-out at Junction of Piccadilly and Cambridge Trenches I 5 d. 0.3.

(b) Via South of Oskar Farm to Junction of Ice Walk and Ibex Reserve.

(c). Along northern end of Wilde Wood to vicinity of Douglas VILLA.

Shown on attached map thus :- A.R ?

The calls for the Brigade Forward Stations after ZERO will be :-

A.R.F – dug out at I 5 d. 0.3.

A.R.G. – Station at Junction of ICE WALK and IBEX RESERVE.

A.R.H. – Station near DOUGLAS VILLA.

"TANKS." No. 9 Company "C" Battalion has been allotted to the 44th and 46th Infantry Brigades, and will co-operate with them in the attack on the BLACK LINE.

The starting point will be immediately South West of the BELLE WAARDEBEEK Stream at I. 4. d 80.95.

The three following general signals will be used by Tanks: and Infantry should know them by heart :-

GREEN DISC ... "Have reached objective"

RED " ... 'Broken down'

WHITE " ... "No enemy in sight."

WATER & RATIONS The following arrangements regarding Water during operations are notified:-

(a) Each man will carry one filled water bottle.

(b) 500 filled Water Bottles per Battalion (extra to establishment) will be dumped in Brigade Dump at A.R.A.

(c). 300 filled petrol tins will be dumped at A.R.A and 50 at A.R.B.

(d) A reserve of 4,000 gallons of water will be

[illegible]

HELL FIRE CORNER [illegible]

[illegible] bottles of troops [illegible] in Y.P.

[illegible]

(6) Initial Water Point at Swimming Bath N.E. corner of YPRES will be the refilling place for [illegible] until advanced waterpoints are working.

(8) Rations for "Z" day (unexpended portion) and "Z" plus 1 day in addition to the iron emergency [illegible] carried on the man by troops in and east of Ypres on "Z" day.

(9) Rations for "Z plus 2" day will be [illegible] and will be dumped [illegible] day in [illegible]

(10) Rations and [illegible] troops west of Ypres at Zero hour will be [illegible] for "Z plus 1" and "Z plus 2" [illegible]

[illegible] will be [illegible] to them.

[illegible] the field [illegible] east [illegible] CHATEAU at Zero plus 6 hours.

It will push forward patrols to the high ground N.E. of KEERSELAARHOEK on the PASSCHENDAELE RIDGE.

[illegible] patrol is also being sent by the 55th [illegible] across the valley of the STROOMBEEK as far as the ZONNEBEKE STADEN LINE near WOLF FARM.

[illegible] Barrett
CAPTAIN
[illegible] 44th Machine Gun Coy.

[illegible] July 1917.

SHEET 28
I & J
SCALE 1 : 5.000
30-6-17
BATTERY POSITIONS
TRENCHES
MACHINE GUNS
TRENCH MORTARS
DUMPS
WAR DIARY.
N
SQUARE FM.
CREY RUIN
LOW FARM
FROST HOUSE
FREZENBERG
ODER HOUSE
OUTPOST
RUPPRECHT FARM
BAVARIA Ho
THE STABLES
EITEL FRITZ FARM
OSKAR FARM
BRITISH FRONT LINE
BILL COTTAGE
DOUGLAS VILLA
A.R.H.
A.R.G.
A.R.C.
A.R.D.
Nth STATION BUILDINGS
SOUTH STATION BUILDINGS
RABBIT VILLA
WILDE WOOD
Lt SCHLOSS +2 GUNS
Lt MARSHALL +2 GUNS
Lt JENKINS +2 GUNS
Lt BOWN +2 GUNS.
Ibex Drive
Ice Walk
Ice Lane
Topo. Sec. I.B. 14

War Diary
Copy No

SECRET.

ADDENDUM No 1. to

Preliminary Instructions by
Captain R. V. Barrett Cdg.
44th Machine Gun Coy

1/ After the capture of the GREEN Line patrols will be pushed forward to seize any tactical points vacated by the enemy up to the RED Line. See attached map. The Divisions on Right and Left are acting in a similar manner. It is not the intention to attack any positions held by the enemy E. of the GREEN Line.

2. At Zero plus 8 hours 30 mins B.G.C. 45 I.B. will push forward posts to the line D 31.d.70.50. – Hill 40 – D 31 d – D 31 a 70.60 – DOCHY FARM – D 14.d.2.4 shown in Brown on map. This line will then become the line of resistance of the Division.

3/ (1). As soon as information has been received that 45th Inf. Bde have established posts on the BROWN Line D 31.d.7.5. – Hill 40 in D 31 d – D 31 a 70.60 – DOCHY FARM – D 14 d 2.4. 8th Bn Seaforth Highlanders will push forward patrols from the ZONNEBEKE – LANGEMARCK Road to the Red Line. These patrols will be supported by the remainder of the Battalion which will not however move forward East of the GREEN Line until information has been received that the 8th Division has established posts on the BROODSEINDE – NIEWEMOLEN Road. When this has been done 8th Seaforth will establish a line of outposts on the RED Line.

(2) Accordingly 8th Seaforth will be prepared to advance from the Green line to the valley in D 16 a by

ZERO plus 7 hours 30 mins.

(3) The Divisional front extends from about D9d 2.5 to D16d 3.4.

(4) In addition to the two Vickers guns (Lt. Marshall) allotted to 8th Seaforth Hrs. the two Reserve guns of 44th M.G. Coy (Lt. JENKINS) will also accompany the Battalion.

3. (1) As soon as it becomes clear that the 8th Division is established on the RED Line orders will be issued by the DIVISION for the Red Line to be occupied by the 44th I.B as the line of Resistance.

(2). On receipt of these orders 44 I.B. will move forward in following orders:-

7th Cameron Highlanders.
8/10th Gordon Highlanders.
9th Black Watch.

Detailed instructions will be issued later.

4. One troop of the N.I. Horse will advance under the orders of B.G.C. 44th I.B from the green Line at ZERO plus 8 hrs 30 mins and will push out patrols to ABRAHAM HEIGHTS (D.15.b) and the high ground about D 12. a. 2.0.

5. The advance beyond the GREEN LINE will not be preceded by a barrage and all available heavy artillery will lift to points not less than 500 yds from and beyond the SEINE - GRAVENSTAFEL - WURST FARM Road at ZERO plus 8 hrs 20 mins.

As soon as the RED Line becomes the line of Resistance the protective barrage will be 300 yds in front of the RED Line

After ZERO plus 8 hrs 30 minutes it will only be put down in the event of an SOS call.

and substitute :-

"2 M.Gs. detailed by the O.C. the half of 225 M.G. Coy attached to the Brigade will be posted in A."

PACK PONIES.

8 Pack Animals will be at A Battery Position I 11 a 6.4 at Zero + 2 hours. Drivers will lead 2 mules as far as the position. Mr. WINN will then detail 2 men from B Section and 2 from "C" Section to lead one pack animal each.

COY HDRS.

Coy Hdrs. from Y/Z night will be at dug-out, Junction of South Lane and the Ypres - Roulers Rly. From Zero + 2 hours Hqtrs will be at WIELTJE [illegible].
Subsequent moves will be notified later.

[illegible signature]
Captain
Cdg. 110th M.G. Coy

25/7/17.

6. 44th and 45th I.B. will establish a [illegible] Post with 9th Division at [illegible] ZONNEBEKE as early as possible. 8th Seaforth Hdrs will detail an Officer with [illegible] for this post.

MOBILE DUMP. 7. [illegible] line Transport of Battalions will be [illegible] about H.16 [illegible] instead of H.17 D. They will move [illegible] on Y/Z night as follows:-

Starting Point. – Cross Roads in H.7 C.

Time. – 10.0 p.m.

Order of [illegible] – 45th 44th – 46th Brigades

Route – H 8 a 5.3 – H 8 d 7.3 – H 9 a 7.5. – Cross Roads in H.16 d

Destination – [illegible] (Eastern half of field)

8. Formation of Divisional Mobile Dump

Captain R. Robertson 10th [illegible] H.L.I. is appointed to command the Divisional Mobile Dump.

The G.S. Limbered Wagons (Complete Turnout) to be detailed by this Brigade will be detailed from the 44th [illegible] by the Brigade T.O.

They will report to O.C. Divisional [illegible] up in the [illegible] field at H.16 d 9.4 at 8 a.m. on Z day.

Limbered wagons will be loaded under arrangements of O.C. Div. Mobile Dump and will be [illegible] at H 16 d.9.4.

RUNNERS. All runners should be instructed to carry messages in their [illegible] hand pockets.

CORRECTION. Page 3. Delete " The two Reserve Machine Guns [illegible] will [illegible] this line "

[illegible] last line and subsequent line on page 4. Delete " The [illegible] [illegible] with Mr. Marshall will be [illegible] in Post 2"

Dan Deary

Machine Gun Barrage.

Preliminary Instructions.

1. It is proposed to employ the Machine Guns on the Corps Front.

(a) To cover the Infantry advance to the Blue Line.

(b) To keep the FREZENBERG Line under fire during the pause on the BLUE Line.

(c) To support the advance on the BLACK Line at the commencement.

(d) As soon as the Black Line is obtained to move up all the barrage machine guns to previously selected places about 2000 yards from the [illegible] GHELUVELT Line in order to support a further advance on the GREEN Line.

2. (1) Trace attached indicates.

RED LINES. The targets to be engaged from the first position.

GREEN LINES. The targets to be engaged from 2nd posn.

BLUE LINES. The targets to be engaged from the 2nd position.

3. ORGANISATION. For simplicity and to facilitate control, the Machine Guns will be organised into Batteries of 8 guns each. Two Batteries form a group and one group will be allotted to each Brigade Front.

4. As soon as the troops reach the BLACK Line the Machine Guns will move forward to the positions shown on the Trace.

The group Commanders will move to forward positions.

5. The guns composing the barrage will consist of:—

The guns composing the Barrage will consist of:-

RIGHT GROUP A Battery 8 guns 44th M.G. Coy.

B Battery 8 guns 47th —"—

The positions of the guns will be as shown the attached trace

Headquarters of Right Group (Capt. Barrett 44th M.G. Coy) I 10 d 5.5.

The Divisional M.G. officer will be with 45th Infantry Brigade

6/ When the troops have reached the Green Line the Machine Guns will form a protective Barrage as shown on the trace, and will be put on in the event of an "S.O.S" call.

7/ The Machine guns will be in position by "Y/Z" night when they will come under the orders of Major WILKINSON. D.M.G.O.

8/ If there is any delay in the operations necessitating an alteration in the M.G. Barrage before the BLACK LINE is reached, the guns of the Right Group will act under the orders of G.O.C. 44th Inf. Bde.

After the BLACK LINE has been reached both groups will come under the tactical control of G.O.C. 45th Inf. Bde.

9/ A further move forward beyond the FREZENBURG ROAD - will then be made to form a S.O.S or protective barrage beyond the Green Line.

10/ Each Battery will be 8 guns and suggested that 3 officers, 2 Sgts, 2 Cpls, 32 Machine Gunners and 16 Carriers.

8 Pack Animals will assist to carry S.A.A etc forward to second position.

12/ Firing and moves will be carried out strictly in accordance with ~~[illegible]~~ FIRE and MOVE Orders attached.

13/ "A" Battery will consist of B and C Sections under the orders of T/LT. WINN [illegible] T/LT. FELL and T/LT. WILSON.

14/ The following equipment is to be at each Barrage position :

130 Boxes S.A.A.

176 Belt Boxes

1 Drum Oil.

16 Petrol Tins Water.

8 Tripod Platforms.

8 Baby Elephants

Aiming Posts

Discs to show Battery Positions.

Wire and Stakes.

Sandbags.

15/ On receiving [illegible] LT. FELL, an N.C.O and 1 runner will go forward to find out the situation and reconnoitre fresh positions at approximately :-

A Battery to the East of Welsh wood

B " " " " Bill Cottage.

Teams should move forward in rounds and be ready to come into ~~action~~ at any moment.

J.K. Barrett Capt.
Comd/ 44 M.G. Coy

M.G. FIRE ORGANISATION ORDER.

No. of Guns.	No. of Battery.	Compositions.	Location.	Firing From	Firing To.	Target.	Rate of Fire.	Remarks.
8	"A"	44th M.G. Coy.	I [illegible] 48.33	0	15 mins	I 6 d 85.88 to I 6 [illegible] 53.33	1 Belt in 4 mins.	Search 400 yds beyond Target. Depression stops to be set for Q.E. of TARGET.
				15 mins	1 hr 5 mins	J 16 [illegible] to D 28 c 90.36	1 Belt per 4 mins.	Search 200 yds beyond Target. Depression stops [illegible] for Q.E. of Target. On S.O.S. open maximum rate on Target for 10 mins. and continue ordinary rate after. ~~Depression stops to be set for Q.E. of Target.~~
				1 hr 6 mins	1 hr 23 mins	J.1.B 46.84 to D 25 d. 11.56.	1 Belt per 4 mins.	Depression stops to be set for Q.E. of Target.
8	A 1.	44th M.G. Coy.	I.6.B. 73.[illegible]			D 26 d 02.80 to D 26 a 76.57		[illegible] one belt as soon as in position. On S.O.S. open maximum rate of fire for 10 mins and continue ordinary rate of fire for [illegible] mins.
				6.08	[illegible].32.	D 26 d. 02.80 to D 26. a. 76.57	1 Belt per 4 mins.	Search 200 yds beyond Target. Depression stops to be set for Q.E. of Target.
				6.33	[illegible].50	D 26. b. 94.37 to D 20. d. 65.02.	Belt per 4 mins.	Search 200 yds beyond Target. Depression stops to be set for Q.E. of Target.
8	A 2.	44th M.G. Coy.	D 28. d. 00.07.	7.33	8.20	[illegible].20 to D 21 34.03.	1 Belt per 4 mins.	Search 200 yds beyond Target. Depression stops to be set for Q.E. of Target. On S.O.S. maximum [illegible] to be opened on Target for 10 mins.

Exhibit 8

Ventry

SECRET

OPERATION ORDER No 44.
by Capt K. V. Barrett
Comdg 44th M.G. Coy – 2-7-17.

1. The following reliefs will take place on the night 2/3 July.
2/Lt A. Marshall and 2/Lt R. Wilson will relieve 2/Lt Brown at St James Trench.
C Section will relieve "B" Sect.
A " teams 3 & 4 will relieve A Sect teams 1 & 2.
Pte Cameron will report at Coy H.Q. to guide up No 3 & 4 teams at 9.0 PM.
B Sect will send down guides 1 per gun team at Coy H.Q. at 12 midnight.
8 belt boxes per gun will be taken over by ingoing teams as well as their trench stores. Lists of Trench Stores taken over to accompany morning report.

K Barrett
Captain
Comdg 44th M.G. Coy

DISTRIBUTION

Copy No 1 — O/C
" " 2 — Adjt
" " 3 — [illegible]
" " 4 — 2/Lt Brown
" " 5 — 2/Lt Marshall
" " 6 — 2/Lt Wilson
" " 7 — } War Diary
" " 8 — }
" " 9 — File

Copy 1.
War Diary

Secret. OPERATION ORDER No. 45
by Capt R. V. Barrett
Comdg 44th M.G. Coy.

8 July 1917.

I. The 44th M.G. Coy will be relieved by the 45th M.G. Coy on the night 8/9 July.

II. GUIDES:-
1 to guide 45th M.G. Coy from Transport lines to REIGSBURG CHATEAU. 4 to guide from REIGSBURG CHATEAU at 10.0 PM to SCHOOL HOUSE; thence 1 per gun (to be at H.Q. at 10.30 PM).

III. On relief, gun teams will come direct to SCHOOL HOUSE where they will deposit their kit, leaving 1 man per gun as loading party. They will then be formed into parties & march to TRANSPORT LINES.

IV. All No. 1s will remain in for 24 hours. They will meet at SCHOOL HOUSE at 10.0 AM 9.7.17 and march down as a party to the TRANSPORT LINES.

V. 2/Lt Brown will go to TRANSPORT LINES and arrange accommodation.

R V Barrett
Capt
Comdg 44 M.G. Coy

DISTRIBUTION
Copy No. 1 - O/C
2 - Adjt
3 - 2/Lt Keel
4 - " Winn
5 - " Wilson
6 - " Brown
7 }
8 } War Diary
9 File

Secret OPERATION ORDER No 46
by Capt H. V. Barrett
Comdg 44 M.G. Coy
9.7.17

I The 44th M.G. Coy will move to the RUBROUCK area on the 10th inst.

II ROUTE March Route to POPERINGHE Station via Road junction G.2.d.2.2. Thence by rail to ARNEKE.

III The Company will pass the Starting point Road junction G.5.d.1.2 at 6.30 AM.

IV Transport will not proceed by rail with Company, but under instructions as issued to T.O.

V DRESS: Full marching order. F.S. Caps to be worn.

VI PARADES:

4.0 AM Reveille
4.30 " Breakfast
5.30 " Coy. marches off.

[signature] for
Capt
Comdg 44 M.G. Coy

Operation Order No 47
by Capt K.V. Barrett
Comdg 44th M.G. Coy
16th July 1917

I B & C Section will move to WINIZEELE Area tomorrow 17.7.17.

II Section will take Section dixies.

III Detail as in warning order.
The Right Half Company will proceed by march route to WINIZEELE area.

PARADES:
4 0AM Reveille
4 30 Breakfast
5 30 Parade

K Barrett
Capt
Comdg 44 MG Coy.

SECRET OPERATION ORDER No 49
by Lieut G. Jenkins
Comdg Left Half 44 M.G. Coy
22 July 1917

I The Half Coy of 46 M.G. Coy & the left half Coy of 44th M.G. Coy will move to L.15. b. 9.1 WATOU area No 1 on 22.7.17

II The Company will pass the starting point of WINNIZEELE cross roads J.17. a. 6.5 at 6.4[illegible]

III ROUTE –
WATOU cross roads K.13. c
– road junction L.13. d. 5.0

PARADES

4.0 AM Reveille
4.30 " Breakfasts
5.30 " Parade

G. Jenkins Lieut
Comdg Left Half Coy

Secret OPERATION ORDER No. 48.
by Lieut G. Jenkins
Comdg. Left Half 44 M.G. Coy

20th July 1917

I The 44th M.G. Coy (Left Half Coy) will move from ROUBROUCK area to WINIZEELE No. 2 area J.3.C.33 on the 21st inst.

II Company will pass the starting point, cross roads VIOLON D'OR H.11.C.8.4 at 5.37 AM

III ROUTE:- ARNEKE — HARDIFORK.

IV DRESS:- Fighting Order with steel helmets on haversacks:

V PARADES:-

3.0 AM Reveille
3.30 - Breakfasts
4.30 - Company Parade
4.45 - Company move off

G. Jenkins Lieut
Comdg Left Half Coy

Secret OPERATION ORDER No. 50.
by Lieut G. Jenkins
Comdg Left Half 44 MG Coy
23. July 1917

I 44th & 46th M.G. Coys (Half Coys) will move to TORONTO CAMP 23 July 1917.
II The Coys will pass the starting point, cross roads L. 11. a. 4.4 at 7.24 AM.
III ROUTE.

Switch Road N of POPERINGHE.

PARADES

5.30AM Reveille
6.0 - Breakfasts
6.45 - Coys Parade
6.50 - Coys move off

G. Jenk
Lieut
Comdg Left Half Coy

Secret Operation Order No 51
by Capt K.V. Barnett
Comdg 44 M.G. Coy.

1 The composite Machine Gun Coy of the 46th Brigade M.G. Coy will relieve 45 M.G. Coy on the night of 19-20 July 1917.

2 Half Coy of the 44th M.G. Coy will relieve 2 guns in WEST LANE & the remaining 6 guns will be in the ECOLE

3 Lieut Munro & 2 guns of 'B' Section will over the guns in WEST LANE Sectional H.Q at I.10.D.5.9.

10 Belt boxes per gun will be taken over from 45th Coy.

Coy Parade 8.15 P.M.
Move off 8.30 .

all petrol Cans & Water Bottles to be filled.

Sgt Glover & 12 men will take over Gas Guard at Coy H.Q. from 45 M.G. Coy immediately on arrival

[signature] 2/Lieut
for Capt
Comdg 44 M.G. Coy

"A" Form.

MESSAGES AND SIGNALS.

Army Form C.2121
(In pads of 100).
No. of Message ....

Prefix .... Code .... m. | Words | Charge

Office of Origin and Service Instructions.

Sent
At .... m.
To ....
By ....

This message is on a/c of:
.... *Service.*
....
(Signature of "Franking Officer.")

Recd. at .... m.
Date ....
From ....
By ....

TO

Sender's Number.	Day of Month.	In reply to Number.	AAA
*			

From
Place
Time

The above may be forwarded as now corrected. (Z)

....
Censor. Signature of Addressor or person authorised to telegraph in his name.

* This line should be erased if not required.

750,000. W 2186—M509. H. W. & V., Ld. 6/16.

O.O. 52 (Cont)

will go to position in South Lane this evening.

8 men will parade and will carry up:—

Gun, Tripod, water and 2 belt Boxes per gun.

1 Sergeant & 8 men of the 225 M.G. Coy will go up, 4 men to each gun. They will carry 8 Belt Boxes per gun — 16 in all.

1 N.C.O & 2 men of [illegible] M.G. Coy & 2 men of 225 Coy will remain with each of the 2 guns. The remainder will return immediately to H.Q^rs.

3 Parade Section will parade with every thing ready to move by 10 pm

4 Details for harassing fire to follow.

W.A. Bell 2/Lieut
for Capt
Comdg 4th M.G. Coy

"A" Form.

MESSAGES AND SIGNALS.

(In pads of ...) No. of Message ....

Prefix .... Code .... m.	Words	Charge	This message is on a/c of:	Recd. at .... m.
Office of Origin and Service Instructions.			.... Service.	Date ....
	Sent			From ....
	At .... m.			
	To			
	By		(Signature of "Franking Officer.")	By ....

TO

Sender's Number.	Day of Month.	In reply to Number.	AAA
*			

From

Place

Time

The above may be forwarded as now corrected. .... Censor.

(Z) Signature of Addressor or person authorised to telegraph in his name.

* This line should be erased if not required.

750,000. W 2186—M509. H. W. & V., Ld. 6/16.

Secret. Operation Order No. 52
by Capt K. V. Barrett
Comdg 44 M.G. Coy.
20/7/17.

1 'C' Section 3 guns of 'C' Section will go to positions in St James Trench this evening to carry out indirect fire. 30 men will parade & carry up:- Gun, tripod, water, 10 belt boxes per gun, and 2 boxes of S.A.A per gun.

2 men of 225 M.G. Coy will go with each gun team & will carry one S.A.A Box each.

3 men of 46 M.G. Coy will go with each team to carry S.A.A.

1 N.C.O. & 2 men of 44 M.G. Coy per gun & 2 men of 225 Coy per gun will remain under orders of Lieut Murray 46 Coy. The remainder will return to H.Q. immediately.

2 'B' Section 2 guns of 'B' Section

"A" Form.

Army Form C.2121
(In pads of 100).

MESSAGES AND SIGNALS.

No. of Message..........

Prefix ....Code............m.

Office of Origin and Service Instructions.

Words | Charge

Sent
At..................m.
To..................
By..................

This message is on a/c of:
..........................*Service.*
(Signature of "Franking Officer.")

Recd. at...............m.
Date...............
From...............
By...............

TO

Sender's Number.	Day of Month.	In reply to Number.	AAA
*			

From
Place
Time

The above may be forwarded as now corrected.

(Z)

..................*Censor.*

Signature of Addressor or person authorised to telegraph in his name.

* This line should be erased if not required.

750,000. W 2186—M509. H. W. & V., Ld. 6/16.

Secret OPERATION ORDER No 53.
by Capt R. V. Barnett
Comdg 44 M.G. Coy
28/7/17

War Diary

Ref. Sheet 28 N.W.
1/20000

B & C Sections of 44 M.G. Coy will move from Bivouac at H 16. d. 1. 2 to the SCHOOL HOUSE on the night of 29/30th July.
The Sections will proceed by F track and will reach the starting point - Road H. 12. C. 0. 1 - Belgian Battery Corner at 10. P.M. The starting line to be cleared by 10. 15 P.M. F track starts at H. 16. d. 2. 8.
2/Lt Wilson & a N.C.O will reconnoitre the route tomorrow.
Company parade 9. 15 P.M.

W.R. Dill Lt
for Capt
Comdg 44 M.G. Coy

DISTRIBUTION

Copies No 1 - Lieut Jenkins
2 - T.O
3 } War Diary
4 }
5 - File.

Secret OPERATION ORDER N° 54
by Capt K.V. Barrett
Comdg 44th M.G. Coy
30/7/17

1 The 44th Infantry Brigade will attack the enemy's positions on the 31st day of July 1917 at 3.50 AM in accordance with Preliminary Instructions previously issued.

11 The guns of the 44th M.G. Coy will cooperate in the assault as laid down in 44th M.G. Coy "Preliminary Instructions"

[illegible]
for Captain
Comdg 44 M.G. Coy

30/7/17.

Instructions regarding War Diaries and Intelligence Summaries are contained in F. S. Regs., Part II. and the Staff Manual respectively. Title pages will be prepared in manuscript.

WAR DIARY
or
~~INTELLIGENCE SUMMARY.~~

(Erase heading not required.)

Army Form C. 2118.

Vol 18

Place	Date	Hour	Summary of Events and Information	Remarks and references to Appendices
			CONFIDENTIAL	
			WAR DIARY	
			OF	
			44th MACHINE GUN COMPANY	
			from August 1st 1917 to August 21st 1917	
			(Volume XIX)	
			[illegible] Capt	

A5834 Wt. W4973/M687 750,000 8/16 D. D. & L. Ltd. Forms/C.2118/13.

Army Form C. 2118.

Instructions regarding War Diaries and Intelligence Summaries are contained in F. S. Regs., Part II. and the Staff Manual respectively. Title pages will be prepared in manuscript.

WAR DIARY
or
INTELLIGENCE SUMMARY.

(Erase heading not required.)

Place	Date	Hour	Summary of Events and Information	Remarks and references to Appendices
YPRES	1.8.17		Counter attack by enemy – driven off with heavy losses. Our forward guns caught enemy advancing in mass, and claim heavy casualties	LSh
	2.8.17		Enemy barrages Black line during the day. Artillery activity on both sides.	LSh
	3.8.17		Relieved by 45th M.G Coy. Coy moved to B[illegible] Camp.	LSh
WINNEZEELE	4.8.17		Moved by bus to WINNEZEELE area.	LSh
	5.8.17		Cleaning guns equipment etc	LSh
	6.8.17		Training and refitting	LSh
	7.8.17		Training and refitting	LSh
	8.8.17		Training and refitting	LSh
	9.8.17		Training	LSh
	10.8.17		Training	LSh
	11.8.17		Training	LSh
	12.8.17		Training	LSh
	13.8.17		Training	LSh
	14.8.17		Training	LSh
	15.8.17		Training	LSh
	16.8.17		Training	LSh
	17.8.17		Training	LSh
POPERINGHE	18.8.17		~~Training~~ Company moved to POPERINGHE. Operation orders attached	LSh

A5834 Wt. W4973/M687 750,000 8/16 D. D. & L. Ltd. Forms/C.2118/13.

Instructions regarding War Diaries and Intelligence Summaries are contained in F. S. Regs., Part II. and the Staff Manual respectively. Title pages will be prepared in manuscript.

WAR DIARY
or
INTELLIGENCE SUMMARY.
(Erase heading not required.)

Army Form C. 2118.

Place	Date	Hour	Summary of Events and Information	Remarks and references to Appendices
POPERINGHE	19.8.17		Company moved to billets in YPRES. Operation Order attached	[illegible]
YPRES	20.8.17		Relieved 41 Machine Gun Company at POMMERN REDOUBT	[illegible]
	21.8.17		Y day. Artillery active on both sides. 2/Lt ERSKINE wounded.	[illegible]
	22.8.17		Z day. Attack on enemys positions at 4.45 am. Held up by Machine Gun fire from block houses. Very little progress – heavy casualties. Preliminary instructions attached	[illegible]
	23.8.17		Great artillery activity.	[illegible]
	24.8.17		Attack on GALLIPOLI FARM by 9th Black Watch unsuccessful.	[illegible]
	25.8.17		Artillery active.	[illegible]
	26.8.17		Enemy still holding out in block houses.	[illegible]
	27.8.17		H.L.I. attacked GALLIPOLI in conjunction with an attack by 61st Division of the left, but unsuccessful	[illegible]
	28.8.17		Great artillery activity	[illegible]
	29.8.17		Artillery active. Relieved by 46 M G Coy.	[illegible]
	30.8.17		Moved to Bivouac Camp. Division relieved by 42nd Division	[illegible]
	31.8.17		Moved to WATTEAU area.	[illegible]

Preliminary Instructions by Lieut E Rogers

Comdg 44th M.G. Coy 20 - August 1917

Ref: Frezenberg Sheet 1/10000.

I The 15th Division will resume the offensive on Z day.
The 61st Division will attack on our left.

II 45th Brigade will be on the Right 44th Inf Bde on the left with the 46th Brigade in Reserve.

III The Northern boundary of the Brigade is from D.19.a.35.45 North of the northern house in Gallipoli to D.14.c.45.60.
The Southern Boundary is from D19c.90.35 along the ZONNEBEK Stream.
The dividing line between Battalions is D.19.a.71 to D20.c 80.55.

IV The objective of the 15th Div runs from the Eastern edge of Gallipoli Copse just to the West of BRETHEN Redoubt & then back to the West of POTSDAM. It is essential that posts should secure the high ground immediately East of the line

V The 44 Bde will attack with:-
8th Seaforths on Right
7th Camerons on left
8/10 Gordons in Support
9th Black Watch in Reserve
and will capture the objective from D20.c7.7 to D14.c.4.7

VI The 44th M.G. Coy will cooperate as follows:-
2 guns B Section under Lt Munro will be attached to 8th Seaforths.
2 guns B Section under 2/Lt Poole will be attached 7th Camerons.
2 guns C Section under 2/Lt Erskine will be attached to 8/10 Gordons.
Remaining 10 guns will be in reserve in Cambridge Trench under orders of O.C 44 M.G. Coy.
Coy. H.Q. will be in Cambridge Trench.

(Cont)

Cont

VII The attack will be supported by the 15th, 16th & 5th Australian Divisional Artilleries who will operate a creeping barrage moving probably at the rate of 100 yards in 5 minutes.

VIII The attack of the Division will be covered by M.G. Barrage, from 32 guns found by 46th & 225th M.G. Companies under the orders of D.M.G.O.

IX Fighting kit to be carried by the man:-

Steel Helmet
Equipment, entrenching tool & carrier.
Respirator & P.H. Helmet.
Mess Tin
Water Bottle
Waterproof Sheet.
Ration for Z and Z plus 1 days & emergency Ration
100 rounds SAA per Vickers gunner.
5 Sandbags.

Per Gun.-

1 Gun.
1 Tripod
2 Petrol Cans
10 Belt boxes.
Condenser & tube & 1st aid Case.

[signature]
Lieut
Comdg 44 M.G. Coy

Secret [illegible] Operation Order No. 53.
by [illegible]
Comdg [illegible] M.G. Coy
19 Aug 19[illegible]

[illegible]

[illegible] M.G. Coy will move to the [illegible]
[illegible] tonight 19 [illegible]

Company Parade at 5.15 PM

Company will [illegible] the [illegible]
[illegible] 200 yds [illegible] fighting
[illegible] with accompanying Sections.

A Section will move [illegible]
[illegible]
[illegible] X [illegible] G. [illegible] 3[illegible]
at 6.15 PM

[illegible]
Lieut
Comdg [illegible] M.G. Coy

Secret

OPERATION ORDER No. 52
by Lieut E. Rogers
Comdg 44 M.G. Coy
17th 8 1917

The Company will move to No. 3 AREA BRANDHOEK by march route.

Company will parade at X. roads in front of Coy H.Q. at 1.30 PM & pass starting point at 2.25 PM

DRESS.

Fighting order with steel helmets strapped to haversacks

March discipline

East of Poperinghe – Proven Rd 500 yards distance will be maintained between units 200 yards between Companies Transport will accompany units at 200 yds distance

E Rogers
Lieut
Comdg 44 M.G. Coy

Instructions regarding War Diaries and Intelligence Summaries are contained in F. S. Regs., Part II. and the Staff Manual respectively. Title pages will be prepared in manuscript.

WAR DIARY
or
INTELLIGENCE SUMMARY.
(Erase heading not required.)

Army Form C. 2118.

Place	Date	Hour	Summary of Events and Information	Remarks and references to Appendices
			Vol 19	
			Confidential	
			(Original)	
			War Diary	
			— of —	
			44th Coy. Machine Gun Corps.	
			from. 1st Sept 1917 to 30th Sept 1917.	
			VOLUME XX	

A5834 Wt. W4973/M687 75,000 8/16 D. D. & L. Ltd. Forms/C.2118/13.

Instructions regarding War Diaries and Intelligence Summaries are contained in F. S. Regs., Part II. and the Staff Manual respectively. Title pages will be prepared in manuscript.

WAR DIARY
or
INTELLIGENCE SUMMARY.
(Erase heading not required.)

Army Form C. 2118.

Place	Date	Hour	Summary of Events and Information	Remarks and references to Appendices
	Sept			
	1		Entrained for Agnez-le-Duisans.	WRJ
LENS 3H 57.68	2.		Arrived at Agnez-le-Duisans	WRJ.
	3.		Training & refitting.	WRJ
	4.		Training & refitting	WRJ
	5.		Training & refitting.	WRJ
C18.c.1.9 57.B N.W.	6.		Moved to Dingwall Camp in Reserve.	WRJ
	7.		Training.	WRJ
	8.		Training.	WRJ
	9.		Training.	WRJ
	10.		Training.	WRJ
	11		Training.	WRJ
	12.		Training.	WRJ
	13.		Training.	WRJ
	14.		Relieved No 45 M.G. Coy in Left Sector Operation Order Attached	WRJ
	15.		Nothing to Report.	WRJ
	16.		Nothing to Report.	WRJ
	17.		Nothing to Report	WRJ
	18.		Nothing to Report.	WRJ
	19.		Considerable hostile Artillery & T.M. Activity.	WRJ
	20.		Nothing to Report	WRJ
	21		Nothing to Report.	WRJ
	22.		Enemy T.Ms and Artillery very active about 4.30 am no Infantry Action followed on this front.	WRJ
	23.		Nothing to Report.	WRJ
	24		Nothing to Report.	WRJ
	25		Nothing to Report	WRJ
	26		Nothing to Report.	WRJ
	27		Nothing to Report.	WRJ
	28		Nothing to Report.	WRJ
	29		Nothing to Report.	WRJ
	30.		Enemy shelled back areas with Gas & HE between 2.0 am & 4.30 am.	

A5834 Wt. W4973/M687 750,000 8/16 D. D. & L. Ltd. Forms/C.2118/13.

War Diary

Secret

OPERATION ORDER No. 54

by Capt K. V. Barrett

Comdg 44 M.G. Coy.

14.9.17

I The 44th M.G. Coy will relieve the 45th Coy on the night 14/15 Sept in the ROEUX Sector.

II A & B Sections will take over positions in the line as per attached list. C and D Sections will be in Reserve near Coy H.Q. H 23.c.7½.9½.

III The Company will move up by train from A5 Station BLANGY.

IV Belt boxes will be taken over.

V Receipts for trench Stores taken over (excluding belt Boxes) will be sent to Coy. H.Q. by 8.0 AM 15th.9.17. with morning report.

K Barrett

Capt

Comdg 44 M.G. C.

Location of Teams

A. 1. CORONA SUPPORT.

2. CORONA SWITCH. (L)

3. CEYLON AVENUE.

4. MOUNT PLEASANT.

B. 5. SCABBARD ALLEY.

6. ROEUX WOOD. (R)

7. " " (L)

8. " X Roads.

14/9/17.

Army Form C. 2118.

Instructions regarding War Diaries and Intelligence Summaries are contained in F. S. Regs., Part II. and the Staff Manual respectively. Title pages will be prepared in manuscript.

WAR DIARY
or
INTELLIGENCE SUMMARY.

(Erase heading not required.)

Vol 20

Place	Date	Hour	Summary of Events and Information	Remarks and references to Appendices
			SECRET	
			CONFIDENTIAL	
			WAR DIARY	
			of	
			44th Machine Gun Company	
			from 1st October 1917 to 31st October 1917	
			(Volume XXI)	

(A7092). Wt. W12839/M1293. 75,0.0. 1/17. D. D. & L., Ltd. Forms/C.2118/14.

WAR DIARY
or
~~INTELLIGENCE SUMMARY.~~
(Erase heading not required.)

Army Form C. 2118.

Instructions regarding War Diaries and Intelligence Summaries are contained in F. S. Regs., Part II. and the Staff Manual respectively. Title pages will be prepared in manuscript.

Place	Date	Hour	Summary of Events and Information	Remarks and references to Appendices
~~[illegible]~~ DINGWALL CAMP	1/10/17		The Coy was relieved in Left Sector of Divisional front by 45th M.G. Coy. Operation Order attached.	SW
	2/10/17		Cleaning & refitting.	SW
	3/10/17		Training	SW
	4/10/17		Training	SW
	5/10/17		Training	SW
	6/10/17		Training.	SW
	7/10/17		Training	SW
	8/10/17		Training	SW
	8/10/17		Preparation for relief.	SW
	9/10/17		The Coy relieved 46th Machine Gun Coy in Right Sector of Divisional front. Operation Order attached.	SW
	10/10/17		Indirect fire carried out on enemy's communications.	SW
	11/10/17		Indirect fire on new trench being dug – also on roads & tracks.	SW
	12/10/17		Indirect fire as usual	SW
	13/10/17		Indirect fire as usual	SW

(A7092). Wt. W12839/M1293. 750,000. 1/17. D. D. & L., Ltd. Forms/C.2118/14.

Army Form C. 2118.

Instructions regarding War Diaries and Intelligence Summaries are contained in F. S. Regs., Part II. and the Staff Manual respectively. Title pages will be prepared in manuscript.

WAR DIARY
or
~~INTELLIGENCE SUMMARY.~~
(Erase heading not required.)

Place	Date	Hour	Summary of Events and Information	Remarks and references to Appendices
ARRAS	14/10/17		Raid by the Division on the right. This Coy did indirect fire with 5" guns. The raid was successful – patrols sent out from our lines were unsuccessful	LSW
	16/10/17		The enemy attempted to raid Division on the left but did not succeed in reaching our wire & suffered heavy casualties	LSW
	16/10/17		Indirect fire carried out on enemy communications	LSW
	17/10/17		Indirect fire	LSW
	18/10/17		Indirect fire	LSW
	19/10/17		Indirect fire	LSW
	20/10/17		Indirect fire – special attention paid to new trenches	LSW
	21/10/17		Indirect fire	LSW
	22/10/17		Indirect fire	LSW
	24/10/17		Indirect fire. Much activity on the left – gas sent over by us.	LSW
	25/10/17		Relieved by 46 Machine Gun Coy in Right Sector. Operation Order attached.	LSW
	26/10/17		Billets in ARRAS. Cleaning	LSW
	27/10/17		Training	LSW
	28/10/17		Training	LSW
	29/10/17		Training	LSW
	30/10/17		Training	LSW
	31/10/17		Training	LSW

(A7092). Wt. W12839/M1293. 75,000. 1/17. D. D. & L., Ltd. Forms/C.2118/14.

Operation Order No 85
by Capt [illegible] M.C.
Comdg 44th MG Coy. 8-10-17

1. The 44th MG Coy will relieve the 45th MG Coy in the right sector 15th Division in the [illegible].
2. A, B & C Sects will take over the positions in the line. D Sect will be in Reserve at WILDERNESS CAMP SOUTH.
3. Teams of 1 NCO & 5 men will go up as [illegible], remainder will be in reserve with D Sect.
4. Guides will meet A, B & C Sects at foot of LANCER LANE at 10.30PM. A, B & C Sects will parade at 8.45PM with 3 limbers for packs & guns.
5. D Sect will parade at 1.45PM with 2 limbers for packs & guns etc.
H.Q. Section will march to Transport lines at 10 AM & will come to trenches by train under orders of [illegible].
6. A, B & C Sections will take over tripods & belt boxes in the line.
D Section will take tripods & 10 belt boxes per gun to WILDERNESS CAMP.

O.O. No. [illegible]

VII. No. 1 will go in [illegible] to relieve [illegible] they will meet guides at foot of LANCER LANE [illegible] 9th inst.

VIII. Reports for Trench Stores will be at H.Q. by 8 AM with morning report.

IX. T.O. will arrange to hand over to 45 M.G. Coy 12 tripods and 114 belt boxes.

X. Rations taken up by teams will be the unexpired portion of the days ration and rations for 10th. C.Q.M.S. to have these ready by 8.30 AM

[signature]
Capt
Comdg [illegible] M.G. Coy

[illegible]

WAR DIARY

OPERATION ORDER No. [illegible]

by Capt [illegible] Barrett. M.C.

Comdg 44 M. G. Coy. 24-[illegible]

I [illegible] M.G. Coy will relieve 44 M.G. Coy on 25th inst [illegible] night 25/26 [illegible]

II Guides 1 per gun [illegible] at [illegible] H.Q at [illegible] Guns that cannot relieve by day will have guides at [illegible]

III The relief teams will move to the bottom of LANCER LANE where they will receive further instructions

IV Horses & limbers for [illegible] parties will be at Left Bde HQ at 3.0 PM.
Horses & limbers for [illegible] parties will be at Left Bde HQ at 9.0 PM.

V Lt Bell will report relief complete from H 86 [illegible] on his way out. Personal [illegible]

VI Trench Stores as per list [illegible] will be handed over & receipts obtained (on attached form)

VII Guides will meet outgoing teams at [illegible] LOCK to guide them to billets in ARRAS

VIII Tripods & belt boxes will be handed over in good condition
Guns & 1st Aids & spare parts etc to be brought out.

IX The petrol cans [illegible] & 20 at H.Q. will be handed over. All others will be brought out [illegible]

X The necessity of carefully handing over [illegible] impressed on all gun team commanders.

XI Lieut Rogers will march "A" [illegible] to billets in ARRAS leaving [illegible] at [illegible] p.m.
2 limbers will be there to convey gun kit, cooks kit & packs.

L. [illegible] Capt
Captain
Comdg 44 M.G. Coy

Instructions regarding War Diaries and Intelligence Summaries are contained in F. S. Regs., Part II. and the Staff Manual respectively. Title pages will be prepared in manuscript.

WAR DIARY
or
INTELLIGENCE SUMMARY.
(Erase heading not required.)

Army Form C. 2118.

Vol 21

Place	Date	Hour	Summary of Events and Information	Remarks and references to Appendices
			CONFIDENTIAL ORIGINAL WAR . DIARY FOR MONTH OF NOVEMBER 1917 OF 44 MACHINE GUN COMPANY VOLUME XXII [signature] Capt o/c 44 M. G. Coy	

A5834 Wt. W4973/M687 750,000 8/16 D. D. & L. Ltd. Forms/C.2118/13.

Instructions regarding War Diaries and Intelligence Summaries are contained in F. S. Regs., Part II. and the Staff Manual respectively. Title pages will be prepared in manuscript.

WAR DIARY
~~or~~
~~INTELLIGENCE SUMMARY.~~
(Erase heading not required.)

Army Form C. 2118.

VOLUME XXIII

Place	Date	Hour	Summary of Events and Information	Remarks and references to Appendices
ARRAS.	Nov 1st		Brigade in Reserve. Training carried out.	
Field	" 2nd		A. D Sects relieved 2 Sects of 45 M. G. Coy in left Sector (ROEUX). 13 guns in line.	
" "	" 3rd		The usual Indirect fire carried out.	
	" 4th		"	
	" 5th		"	
	" 6th		"	
	" 7th		"	
	" 8th		"	
	" 9th		"	
	" 10th		"	
	" 11th		"	
	" 12th		Enemy heavily bombarded FAMPOUX & H13c with Gas shells 3.30AM – 5.0AM	
	" 13th		" " " " H13b " " " 2.30AM – 4.0AM	
			The usual Indirect fire carried out	
	" 14th		" " " " "	
	" 15th		" " " " " 7.30PM 61 Div carried out a raid.	
	" 16th		" " " " " 4.30AM 47 Div "	
	" 17th		Vickers guns co-operated with Artillery in covering fire for raid on Enemy trench by 8(S) R. SEAFORTH HLDRS 44 I Bde at 4.30 AM. 1 Prisoner taken.	
	" 18th		Coy relieved in left Sector by 46 M. G. Coy & moved to Rest billets in ARRAS.	

A5834 Wt. W4973/M687 750,000 8/16 D. D. & L. Ltd. Forms/C.2118/13.

"Instructions regarding War Diaries and Intelligence Summaries are contained in F. S. Regs., Part II. and the Staff Manual respectively. Title pages will be prepared in manuscript.

WAR DIARY

-or-

~~INTELLIGENCE SUMMARY.~~

(Erase heading not required.)

Army Form C. 2118.

Place	Date	Hour	Summary of Events and Information	Remarks and references to Appendices
ARRAS.	Nov 19		Cleaning of Guns, kits etc	
	" 20		16 Guns carried out barrage fire. Embussed at 2.30AM. 32,000 rds expended. ZERO hour 6.0AM. Ceased fire at 6.20AM. Arrived back in billets 8.15AM. No casualties	
	" 21		Training	
	" 22		" "	
	" 23		" "	
	" 24		" "	
	" 25		" "	
FIELD	" 26		Coy relieved 45 M.G. Coy in Right sector. Indirect fire carried out	
	" 27		Indirect fire carried out.	
	" 28		8 guns in line relieved by 11 M.G. Coy. Coy moved to billets in ARRAS	
ARRAS	" 29		Cleaning of Guns, kit etc.	
	" 30		Training	

A5834 Wt. W4973/M687 750,000 8/16 D. D. & L. Ltd. Forms/C.2118/13.

Instructions regarding War Diaries and Intelligence Summaries are contained in F. S. Regs., Part II. and the Staff Manual respectively. Title pages will be prepared in manuscript.

~~WAR DIARY~~
or
~~INTELLIGENCE SUMMARY~~.
(Erase heading not required.)

Army Form C. 2118.

Vol 22

Place	Date	Hour	Summary of Events and Information	Remarks and references to Appendices
			War Diary - of - 44th Machine Gun Coy. for DECEMBER 1917 VOL XXIII (Original)	

A5834 Wt. W4973/M687 750,000 8/16 D. D. & L. Ltd. Forms/C.2118/13.

Instructions regarding War Diaries and Intelligence Summaries are contained in F. S. Regs., Part II. and the Staff Manual respectively. Title pages will be prepared in manuscript.

WAR DIARY
or
~~INTELLIGENCE SUMMARY.~~
(Erase heading not required.)

DEC 1917

VOL XXIII

Army Form C. 2118.

Place	Date DEC	Hour	Summary of Events and Information	Remarks and references to Appendices
	1st		44th M.G. Coy relieved 45th M.G. Coy in Left Sector 15th Divisional Front. O.O. 61 attached	
	2nd		Indirect fire carried out on enemy trenches & tracks. Enemy artillery shelled vicinity of B.H.Q. for 3 hours	
	3rd		Indirect fire carried out. Nothing else to report	
	4th		" " " " "	
	5th		" " " " "	
	6th		" " " " "	
	7th		" " " " "	
	8th		" " " " "	
	9th		" " " Enemy artillery very active.	
	10th		" " "	
	11th		" " "	
	12th		" " "	
	13th		" " "	
	14th		" " "	
	15th			
	17th		Relieved by 46th M.G. Coy. O.O. 62 attached. Gun teams moved into Corps line (Divisional reserve) H.Q. moved to billets in Rue de Turenne Arras.	
	16th		Nothing to report.	
	18th		" "	
	19th		" "	
	20th		Guns in Divisional reserve moved back to reserve billets in Baudimont Barracks ARRAS	
	21st		Nothing to report.	
	22nd		44th M.G. Coy relieved 45th M.G. Coy in the right sector 15th Divisional front.	
	23rd		Nothing to report.	
	24th		Indirect fire carried out on enemy communication	
	25th		" " " "	
	26th		" " " "	
	27th		" " " "	
	28th		" " " "	
	29th		" " " "	
	30th		" " " "	
	31st		" " " "	

Instructions regarding War Diaries and Intelligence Summaries are contained in F. S. Regs., Part II. and the Staff Manual respectively. Title pages will be prepared in manuscript.

WAR DIARY
or
~~INTELLIGENCE SUMMARY.~~
(Erase heading not required.)

Army Form C. 2118.

Vol 23

Place	Date	Hour	Summary of Events and Information	Remarks and references to Appendices
			CONFIDENTIAL	
			WAR DIARY	
			– of –	
			44th M G Coy	
			FROM 1st JAN. 1918 TO 31st JAN 1918	
			VOLUME XXIV (Original Copy)	

[signature] Lieut
o/c 44 M G Coy

A5834 Wt. W4973/M687 750,000 8/16 D. D. & L. Ltd. Forms/C.2118/13.

VOL.ᵐ XXIV

WAR DIARY

or

~~INTELLIGENCE SUMMARY.~~

(Erase heading not required.)

Army Form C. 2118.

44ᵗʰ M. G. Coy

Instructions regarding War Diaries and Intelligence Summaries are contained in F. S. Regs., Part II. and the Staff Manual respectively. Title pages will be prepared in manuscript.

Place	Date JAN 1918	Hour	Summary of Events and Information	Remarks and references to Appendices
	1st		Indirect fire carried out on enemy communication etc.	
	2nd		Company relieved by the 2nd Coy M.G. Guards in the Rt Sector	LSW
			" moved into billets in ARRAS.	LSW
	3rd		Cleaning gun kit and personal equipment.	LSW
	4th		Training carried out.	LSW
	5th		Inspection of Company by G.O.C. 44th Inf Bde in G.20.a	LSW
	6th		Divine Service	LSW
	7th		Training - Company - Arms - Squad & Gun Drill	LSW
	8th		— " —	LSW
	9th		— " —	LSW
	10th		— " —	LSW
	11th		— " —	LSW
	12th		Route March	LSW
	13th		Divine Services	LSW
	14th		Training.	LSW
	15th		Scheme - Practicing fortification of shell hole.	LSW
	16th		Training	LSW
	17th		— " —	LSW
	18th		— " —	LSW
	19th		Inspection by G.O.C. 44th Inf Bde	LSW

A5834 Wt. W4973/M687 750,000 8/16 D. D. & L. Ltd. Forms/C.2118/13.

VOL XXIV

Army Form C. 2118.

Instructions regarding War Diaries and Intelligence Summaries are contained in F. S. Regs., Part II. and the Staff Manual respectively. Title pages will be prepared in manuscript.

WAR DIARY

or

~~INTELLIGENCE SUMMARY.~~

(Erase heading not required.)

44th M.G. Coy

Place	Date	Hour	Summary of Events and Information	Remarks and references to Appendices
	Jan 1918			
	20th		Divine Service	
	21st		Range practice.	
	22nd		'C' Sect on scheme with 8/10 Gordon Hrs.	
			Remainder of Company on Company and gun drill	
	23rd		D Sect with 7th Cameron Hrs on scheme	
			Remainder of Coy doing MG Barrage drill	
	24th		A 'C' & 'D' Section on Bde Tactical Exercise	
			'B' Sect attached to 8th Seaforth Hrs for scheme	
	25th		B. C & D Section on Bde Scheme	
			'A' Sect with 9th Royal Hgrs on scheme	
	26th		All Section on 44th Inf Bde Scheme	
	27th		Divine Service	
	28th		Training – firing on Range	
	29th		Practicing defence of 5 Sect Sub position	
			D. Sect with 7th Cameron Hrs on scheme	
	30th		B C & D Section Range	
			A Section attached 9th Royal Hgrs for scheme	
	31st		Bde scheme A Sect with 9th Royal Hgrs – B Sect with 8th Seaforth Hgrs	
			C & D Section as Barrage Batteries	

A5834 Wt. W4973/M687 750,000 8/16 D. D. & L. Ltd. Forms/C.2118/13.

3. Guides, one per gun, will be at the Triple Arch by 2 p.m. on the 2nd inst. — they will report at Coy Hqrs not later than 1.30. p.m. Guides from No 1, K, L, M posts, will be at the steps where INVERNESS TRENCH cuts the FEUCHY – FAMPOUX road — H 23 d 0.50 Lt. FELL will meet the Guards officer there.

4. For the relief, guns will be grouped as follows:–
2, 3, 4, 5, 6, 7. and 11, 10, 12, 13.
and 1, K, L, M.

5. As far as possible the relief will be carried out in day light — those teams which cannot be relieved in day light will remain at Headquarters in CRETE TRENCH till dusk.
On relief, teams will move to Headquarters and report.

6 On the night 2/3rd the Coy will be billetted in the RUE DE TURENNE.

Lt G. Perkins will arrange to take over billets from Area Commandant.

7. T.O. will draw from T.O. 2nd Coy M.G. Guards 112 belt boxes.

8. Limbers will be required on the 2nd inst as follows:–

1 limber for two Reserve guns, K.L.M posts and Headquarters to be at Stone Dump PAMPOUX – FEUCHY road at 3.30 pm.

1 limber for 6.7.10.11.12.13 Guns at 4.30 pm same place

1 limber for 1.2.3.4.5. Guns at 6 pm same place

Horses for Capt Barrett, Lts Winn, Smith at 6 pm same place
T.O. will see that all drivers know these loads and do not go before the whole load is on
T.O. will bring all spare gun kit

and belt boxes to Coy billets at 10. am on the 3rd.

9. Receipts must be obtained as to condition of Gas blankets, & condition of dugouts in the line – a space is provided for this on the back of the Trench Store list issued.

10. On no account must men be allowed to straggle back – they must wait until a party of at least 20 is collected & march back under the senior N.C.O. – strict march discipline will be observed.

11. The Details billet is to be handed over to the Area Commandant on the morning of the 2nd inst.

12. Acknowledge.

K Barrett
MC Capt.
Cmdg. [illegible] Machine Gun Coy

1/1/18

War Diary

Operation Order No 1
by
Capt K. V. Barrett M.C.
Cmdg 44th Machine Gun Company.

1. The 2nd Coy Machine Gun Guards will relieve the 44th M.G Coy in the Right Sector, Divisional Front on the night 2/3rd January 1918.

2 All trench Stores will be handed over & receipts obtained – receipts on the forms supplied will be handed to Coy. Orderly Room by 9 am on the 3rd inst.
In addition 8 belt boxes per gun in the line will be handed over in good condition.
One petrol can per gun will be handed over.

OPERATION ORDER No. 65

by Lieut Rogers
Cmdg 44th MG Coy

1. 4 Guns of 45th MG Coy and 2 of 225 MG Coy will relieve 6 guns of 44th MG Coy on the night 9/10 Feb 1918.
2. 45th Coy will relieve teams in O.2, R.8, I 5 and I.6.. 225th Coy will relieve teams in I 3 & I 4.
3. Guides to be at Coy H.Q. by 2 PM. 14 Belt Boxes & all Trench Stores to be handed over and receipts taken.
4. On relief teams will move to Coy HQrs for further orders.
5. Lieut [illegible] to report at Coy HQ on relief.

[illegible]
Lieut
O/C 44th MG Coy

Confidential

Vol 24

WAR DIARY

— of —

44th MACHINE GUN COMPANY.

"A" Coy. 15th Batt. M.G.C.

FROM 1st FEBRUARY 1918 TO 28th FEBRUARY 1918.

VOL. XXV

Original COPY.

[illegible] Lieut.
O.C. "A" Coy. 15th Batt. M.G.C.

Army Form C. 2118.

WAR DIARY
~~or~~
~~INTELLIGENCE SUMMARY.~~
(Erase heading not required.)

Instructions regarding War Diaries and Intelligence Summaries are contained in F. S. Regs., Part II. and the Staff Manual respectively. Title pages will be prepared in manuscript.

FEBRUARY 1918 — VOL XXV — A Coy 15th Batt MGC

Place	Date	Hour	Summary of Events and Information	Remarks and references to Appendices
	1st		Training carried out in Reserve area.	LSW
	2nd		Range Practice.	LSW
	3rd		Divine Service.	LSW
	4th		Training.	
	5th		Range practice.	LSW
	6th		44th Coy relieved 11 guns of 13 MG Coy and 4 guns of 234 MG Coy in the line Right Section O.O.64 and addendum No 1 attached	LSW
	7th		Indirect fire carried out on enemy communications.	
	8th		— — —	LSW
	9th		6 team relieved in the line by 4 team of 45 MG Coy and 2 of 225 MG Coy. O.O.65 attached	
	10th		Indirect fire carried out. Training carried out by team in reserve.	LSW
	11th		— — —	
	12th		— — —	LSW
	13th		— — —	
	14th		— — —	
	15th		— — —	
	16th		— — —	
	17th		— — —	
	18th		— — — 6 guns in the line relieved by guns from Reserve, at Bois des Boeufs. Training carried out by team in Reserve	O.O.66 LSW
	19th		— — —	LSW
	20th		— — —	
	21st		— — — Raid on the enemy's front line trenches carried out by 7th Cameron Hrs	
	22nd		in cooperation with artillery and M.G.s O.O.67 MG/57/5 attached	LSW
	23rd		Inter team relief O.O.68 attached.	
	24th		Indirect fire carried out on enemy's tracks and communications. Training for team in reserve.	
	25th		— — —	LSW
	26th		— — —	
	27th		— — —	
	28th		— — —	

A5834 Wt. W4973/M687 750,000 8/16 D. D. & L. Ltd. Forms/C.2118/13.

War Diary

Secret

Operation Order No. 64
by Lt. E. Rogers
Comdg 44 M.G. Coy.

I The 44 M.G. Coy will relieve 11 guns of the 12th M.G. Coy and 4 guns of 23rd M.G. Coy in the morning and evening respectively of 6th inst (W.D.)

II Guides.- Guides will meet all teams with exception of 9-10-11-12 at junction of DIRK TR and CAMBRAI ROAD [illegible] at 11 AM.

III Reliefs as far as possible will be carried out in daylight

IV Guides will meet 9-10-11-12 at Coy H.Q. at 4.5 PM.

V 14 belt boxes per gun will be taken over at each position. List of Trench Stores taken over will reach Coy H.Q. at 9 AM 7th inst.

VI Gun boxes & Belt filling machines will not be taken into the trenches but returned to Transport Lines by 6 PM - 5th inst. Tripods will be taken.

VII 4 Limbers will be loaded:-

(A) No 1 to contain gun kit of No 7. 8. 13. 14 & 15 teams. These teams & limber will parade at 8.30 AM and will march to junction DIRK TR and CAMBRAI RD via Cambrai Road reaching this position by 11. 0 AM.

(B) No 2 to contain gun kit of 1 - 2. 3. 4 - 5 & 6 teams and to reach same point by same route by 11.15 AM.

(C) No 3 to contain gun kit of 9-10. 11. 12 & 16 teams, and to reach same point by same route by 11.30 AM.

(D) No 4 to contain H.Q. kit and will go by [illegible] route under T.O. parading at 9.15 AM

VIII Sgt Caddick will arrange for 1 runner to be attached to [illegible]; Poole; [illegible] and Smith. The remainder of H.Q will march with H-Q limber.

IX Sections will report relief complete by outgoing teams.

X [illegible] will arrange to hand over billets to Billet warden at 8 AM on the 6th inst and see that they are left in a clean condition

XI No 1 of each team will parade under Sgt Caddick and proceed to transport lines of 12 M.G. Coy by 12 noon - 5th inst to report at Coy H.Q of 12 M.G. Coy. Each man will have in his possession 24 ~~days~~ hours rations and chit as to the position he is to take over.

XII T.O will arrange to collect & store all surplus kit i.e. Blankets, packs, officers valises etc.

All packs to be clear of billets by 6 PM - 5th inst.
" Blankets " " " " 7.30 AM — 6th "

T.O will arrange to ~~[illegible]~~ hand over to 12 M.G. Coy 154 belt boxes
" " " " " " " 23rd " 56 " "
on evening of 6th inst on receipt of orders from OC 44 M.G. Coy.

E. Rogers
Lieut
Comdg 44 M.G. Coy

No. 44
MACHINE GUN
COMPANY.
No.............
Date...........

Secret

ADDENDUM No. 1

TO 44 M.G. Coy 0.0. 64

GUN POSITION	GROUP	OFFICER	OFFICERS DUGOUT	Relief	TEAMS	REMARKS
I 1 2 3 4 R 1 2	A	Lt Jenkins	"B" Strong Point		No. 1 2 3 4 5 6	
R 3 4 5	B	2/Lt Poole	R 3		13 14 15	mounted only at night no movement by day
R 6 7 I 5 6	C	2/Lt Littlejohn	Dugout in VINE AVE 0.7.a.3.7		9 10 11 12	no movement by day no fires at emplacements but only in dugouts
R. 8 0.2	D	2/Lt Smith	R 8		7 8	
Coy H.Q N.10.a.9.60 approx	H.Q				16	

14 belt boxes per Gun

5 boxes of S.A.A

M.G. SAA dump at junction of FORK RES and VINE AVE.

Lieut

O.C. 44 M.G. Coy.

SECRET

OPERATION ORDER No 66
BY LIEUT E. ROGERS,
COMDG 44th M.G. COY.

Copy 8
War Diary

I The 6 Reserve teams in BOIS DE BOEUFS Camp will relieve 6 teams in the line on the night 18/19 Feb. 1918.

II Table of relief will be as follows:-

No Team		No Team		Position
3	will relieve	13	at	R3
4	" "	14	"	R5
7	" "	6	"	R2
8	" "	15	"	R4
11	" "	9	"	R6
12	" "	10	"	R7.

Teams will take up guns and first aids – Tripods will be handed over.
No 11 Team will take over gun from No. 9 Team.

III GUIDES – Guides to be at LES FOSSES FARM at 6 PM.

IV Trench Stores & positions to be carefully handed over.

V On relief the relieved teams will move direct to BOIS DE BOEUFS Camp.

VI Relief complete to be reported to the Office. When all teams are relieved 2/Lt Poole and 2/Lt Littlejohn will interchange. The former taking over R.6 and R7 and the latter R.3, R.4, R.5.

VII ACKNOWLEDGE.

DISTRIBUTION

Copy No 1 – O/C
" 2 – 2/Lt Taylor
" 3 – " Poole
" 4 – " Littlejohn
" 5 – " Smith
Copy No 6 – C.S.M.
" 7 – C.Q.M.S.
" 8 – } War
" 9 – } Diary
10 – File

E. Rogers
LIEUT
COMDG No 44 Coy. M.G. Corps

SECRET

Copy No 8
M.G.S. 2/5
21-2-1918.

Operation Order No 67
By O.C. 44th M.G. Coy.

Ref. 44th I.B.O No 236

1. 12 guns of the 44th M.G. Coy divided into two Batteries:-
"A" 8 guns N.12.d.55.30.
"B" 4 " O.7.d.48.90.
and 8 " of 225th M.G.Coy at N.12.b.57.75.
will barrage the enemy lines as per attached table.

2. Teams will be composed of 1 N.C.O and 4 men and 1 officer to each battery of 4 guns.

3. The guns, tripods, 96 belt boxes, clinometers belonging to the 225th M.G.Coy can be taken by limber to LES FOSSES FARM & then man handled to barrage positions at N.12.b.57.75.

4. The guns, tripods, 144 belt boxes clinometers of the 44th M.G.Coy will be taken by limber to LES FOSSES FARM where it will be met at an hour notified later and man handled to barrage positions.

5. 2/Lts. and TAYLOR will be in command of "A" battery, Lt WINN in Command of "B" Battery. Barrage charts will be issued to officers concerned.

6. Officers will check & satisfy themselves that the proper direction & elevation is put on each gun & tripod firmly clamped up.

7. Rate of fire will be carried out as per programme.

8. Guns & ammunition must be thoroughly overhauled before being taken to the line & barrels must be new if possible.

9. After the barrage is finished the gun teams will pick up their gun gear, tripods, T bases & take them to LES FOSSES FARM where a limber will be in waiting. The formation of the emplacement being broken up before leaving.

10. ZERO hour will be notified later.

Copies to

1. D.M.G.O — 2. O.C. 225 M.G.Coy
3. Lt. WINN — 4. 2/Lt TAYLOR
5. 2/Lt — 6. " NUTTING
7. 2/Lt — 8. 2nd i/c.
9. File

[signature] Lieut
O/C 44th M.G. Coy.

Secret.

Operation Order No. 68
by O.C. 44th M.G. Coy

Copy 8

War Diary

Inter team reliefs will take place on night 23/24th Feby 1918.
Teams will take over Tripods & 14 belt boxes only, unless otherwise mentioned.

RIGHT GROUP

2/Lt Taylor

POSITION	PRESENT TEAM	NEW TEAM
I 1	2.	6.
I 2	1	9.
R.2	7	10.
X1.	16	13.

No 13 team will take over gun in addition to other kit.
" 10 " " " " " " " " " "

CENTRE GROUP

Lt. WINN

POSITION	PRESENT TEAM	NEW TEAM
R.4	8	14
R.5	4	15

T.O will arrange for limber to be at BOIS de BOEUF CAMP at 5.PM 23rd inst.
This limber will withdraw to BROWN LINE where it will await relieved teams who will march to BOIS DE BOEUFS CAMP
Guides will meet teams at LES FOSSES FARM at 6.0PM
LISTS of Trench Stores taken over will be rendered to GROUP COMMANDERS by 6 A.M. 24th inst.

TABLE of RELIEFS.

POSITION	GARRISON	RELIEVING TEAM	OFFICER	POSITION OF RELIEVED TEAM.	REMARKS.
I 1	2	6		Bois DE BOEUFS Camp	
I2	1	9	2/Lt TAYLOR	—do—	
R1	5				
R2	7	10		Bois de BOEUFS. Camp	Take over gun
R3	3				
R4	8	14	Lt WINN	BOIS de BOEUFS Camp	
R5	4	15		Bois de BOEUFS Camp	
R6	11		Lt NUTTING		
R7	12				
X1	16	13	2/Lt TAYLOR	Bois de BOEUFS Camp	Take over gun

Copies to

1 O/C
2. Lt WINN
3 " TAYLOR
4 " NUTTING
5 " POOLE
6 T.O
7, 8 } WAR DIARY

John Blundell[?] Lieut
Comdg 44th Coy M.G.C.

www.ingramcontent.com/pod-product-compliance
Lightning Source LLC
Chambersburg PA
CBHW080849230426
43662CB00013B/2061